TRAPPED IN THE BUBBLE

JOHN ROBINSON

TRAPPED IN THE BUBBLE

iSeebookz Publishing
Suite 137B Commerce Ave #300
Lagrange GA 30241

Cover Design: Y.D. Rowland
Editor : Nicole Dixon
Interior Layout: iSeebookz Publishing services

ISBN 979-8-9917114-1-8

First Edition
10 9 8 7 6 5 4 3 2 1

PUBLISHER'S THOUGHTS

In Honor of a Legacy Unseen

Mr. Robinson, you are an inspiration like Mr. Rhynes—fueled by a will and determination that cannot be overlooked. Knowing you, reading your story, and listening to your voice has been a reminder of what true endurance looks like. As a cancer survivor and as someone who has endured more than most, your journey speaks volumes.

As someone personally facing a rare and unexplained medical condition, I find strength in your story. Life is not without challenge—but becoming something more, despite the odds, takes mental fortitude. Your life is a testament to overcoming—reminding all of us who carry our own crosses that purpose still waits on the other side of pain.

And yet, there's more to your story.

Before Chicken Scratch could be written... before the victories and the legacy... There was someone who helped shape the man you became. This book is about him. A quiet force. A guide in the shadows. A man whose impact may never make headlines, but helped form the foundation of your becoming.

Yes—strength through suffering, power through remembering.
The words of my youth quoted within this book...Nothing
from nothing leaves nothing. Has meaning.

I'm just as moved by this book as I was by Chicken Scratch. Thank you for allowing iSeeBookz Publishing to share these voices with the world. Stories like this matter. They remind us why we're here—and that we're not alone. You never questioned God- and in doing so, you've shown that this life is not only to be endured—but lived fully, and poured out as a blessing to others.

With great respect,
— *iSeeBookz Publishing, LLC*

PUBLISHER'S THOUGHTS

INTRO FROM THE AUTHOR

In this part of my life story, some names have been changed to protect the innocent. I'm John Robinson. I've been diagnosed with terminal cancer, and I'm currently in remission.Life is a struggle at times, but still, it's all good. That was over 14 years ago, and I'm still dedicating the rest of my life to God and serving my fellow man.

This is the beginning of a true story I'm about to tell. A story trying to define how the characters became who they were as they stood on the revolving slopes of time. A single fish drowning by the treacherous currents of a raging sea. Let's face it: we are blind swimmers in the sea of time, which has no banks or shores.

As we drift into the deep corridors of our minds, let's focus on humanity and its activities, how humanity reacts to issues and events, living in clusters, on cells of land, such as nations.

Is it a hunger that drives it, constantly devouring and consuming, feeding on the feeble? Hearts filled with vile greed and hatred, minds motivated to rule and be governed by nothing when it comes to treachery.

The heart of man is as big as the nerve of the conductivity of his conscience, of how he thinks. Some seem to have no conscience regarding the results of a decision made by the mind. Even though it paralyzes humanity from the shock of the action rendered by a decision. Like killing a massive portion of the population by race, class, and gender, "how potent is that?"

The complexity of studying a mind like Adolf Hitler, Napoleon, and Idi Amin. They were all reckless swimmers in this vast river of time, and they scarred it with an ugly bruise that forever lingers in the minds of all men, women, and children who are mature enough to comprehend it.

Minds like Putin of Russia, invading Ukraine, creating a trigger for World War III, threatening a lightning-fast response if any nation interfered, ramping and raging, selling war tickets against the world superpowers. Something that Satan himself would provoke. A war in such an inhumane manner, not realizing the after-effects on all life forms on the planet. This is our home, a home for humanity, something that God made in peace. The gravity of the weight and magnitude of the harm will always be recorded in the archives of history.

It seems like our world is on a tremendous pivoting merry-go-round from one tragedy to another. The people of Ukraine are suffering as in the days of the old Exodus. Putin could start the most horrific war that the world of mankind has ever seen since its formation. Just imagine a radioactive fallout worldwide. How horrifying it would be for those clouds to move around the world.

According to the weather patterns, it seems like men would realize the effects of nuclear physics. Pushing the Earth backward and forward almost from its axis and upsetting the balance of nature, creating tsunamis. This would be a dreadful place for all living creatures, especially man.

Putin is a marked man with a price upon his head. Society hates him as much as he hates society. The only thing is that Putin has the most nuclear warheads on the planet. The problem he has is America, the most powerful nation on Earth. When America responded with the flexibility of imposing sanctions on a scale, it afflicted the entire nation of Russia, crippling it so that it could not function as it usually would. President Biden of the United States could not afford to get America on the front line of fire, even though it was tempting to aid the people of Ukraine. Because that would be a direct confrontation with Russia and all its allies, like China, the Dragon.

Then the Eagle and the Dragon and their angels will rumble, shaking the Earth on a global scale. The entire world would be like Hiroshima after the atomic bomb fell upon it.

President Joe Biden really had to measure the greater cost of life, a nation, and the world. We realize that it is a hard decision when you watch little children and elderly people die simply for the craving of power by a tyrant. The television stations in 2024 were flooded with the news of the horrific deaths of so many. 3.7 million people were displaced, fleeing to neighboring countries to survive Putin.

This affected world economies, causing fuel prices to skyrocket. This is a profoundly deep moral standard of mankind's distinction between man and beast. His intellectual ability to survive was based on the decision of World War III.

We, the people of the Supreme Statute of the United States, are enduring a tough life; citizens can't even get money from an ATM because Visa and Master Card don't work anymore.

The Bible speaks about the children of the Nephilim. They are the children of the fallen Angels. Perhaps men like Hitler, Napoleon, and Putin are generationally the bloodline descendants of a people born without a conscience who do not care for the creation of this paradise for man. The only planet in our solar system fit for humanity is now plagued with wars and rumors of wars.

In 2020, we were plagued by viruses. COVID-19 is something that changed our outlook on life. Where did it come from? Did it come from bats or some remote lab in China? Or did it come from the sea because of global warming? Wherever it came from and all its strains, it reaped havoc on the world.

It looks like God spoke to the world and got our undivided attention. For many believers of faith, it came from God to bring about an atonement. Wherever it came from, it's now here. Schools, businesses, churches, and restaurants were shut down, doors closed, and hospitals packed beyond capacity. Hundreds of thousands of people died and are still dying. Look into India and how a new deadly strain killed in 2021. It is and was very scary. Not to mention that another strain of the virus emerged that was deadlier than the first, and it spread very rapidly.

Perhaps this is one of many things that will plague our world, especially America. Looking back over history on a worldwide scale, we see that all nations defied the will of God. They were involved in the destruction of our planet through hate and greed, to the point of slavery, the murder of a nation of people, and the taking of their land. They dropped atomic bombs on cities in Japan and crystallized the ground of direct impact. It caused people, buildings, and bridges to vaporize and vanish in thin air. Shadow images burned on the pavement of children, never knowing they were about to be vaporized by a brilliant light of horrific results.

Yes, my mind wonders if this is the result of the demonic spirits that haunt mankind, and his vile and wicked ways cause me to tremble. But someday, the mighty man shall fall. Because one day, he will realize that we all age and die. It seems like all of mankind is drifting deeper and deeper into the darkness.

Men of power are talking about a war on such a scale that makes me tremble to even write these words, a nuclear war on a global scale. Pumping radiation from one side of the globe to the other, thus spreading the fallout, the rain mud from the clouds that run upon the walls of buildings; horrifying is the word. Just think, all this is from the advancing mind of man.

As I sit here writing this, it brings to mind the horrors and nightmares of how it all came about. The fountain of wealth is a land of untapped resources, such as coal, gold, massive amounts of land, natural resources, and free opportunity. Being free-born and having a good rapport in a land without laws and no governing body, stepping in a westward course due east to find the new land of promise. A nation that one day would rise to become a world superpower. A nation that would stand by Israel to defend it from the rest of the religious world. When most of the Islamic world is against Israel because of a simple belief in the deity. Just imagine a peaceful world, can you see it? How can it be when the leader on every continent hopes to achieve the elements of nuclear power? The superpower nation of today, because of its military strength, is the United States of America, and it stands to defend Israel against the rest of the world. What they do know is that death is the playmate, and it's just ticking day by day, waiting to go off. *What's up with that?*

European theology has exploited the lives of every nation on earth, playing war games of the mind, flexing its muscles of intent all over the world, and flaunting its dominance over the rest of the world. America is a miracle in the eyes of many, especially third-world countries. They see this nation as a God-sent place, unaware that the present conditions of their nation are the results of America's national influence globally.

May God bless America and the new Justice who took her place on the Bench as the first Black woman to sit on the Supreme Court of the United States of America on April 2nd, 2022.

How beautiful and sweet the sound, the way the words paint a picture as gloomy as its majestic skies. But when the veil is uncovered, and the ugly truth is revealed, that is based upon factual truths of hideous events, such as a Bloody Trail of Tears.

I didn't really want to get into this, but I wanted to set the tone and show how the characters I'm writing about became who they are. Maybe the reader will recognize the sign of the trait that has forever scarred Black America.

It started with the first act, a deception, fooling the native Indians into believing they come in PEACE. My friend, see when the pilgrims first landed on the native soil, they were strangers in a strange foreign land. They didn't know anyone, so they stumbled upon these strangely dressed people. To the Indians, they appeared the same, but both were humble to each other. Neither had ever seen such strange beings; one arrived from the sea, and the other emerged from this thick green forest with towering trees. Dressed in their common attire, the pilgrims looked even stranger, with blue eyes, red and blond, black, and even silver-looking hair. These people were indeed different in appearance: one had huge ships anchored out at sea, while the others had a paradise to explore.

So, they befriended each other and kept the truce for years. The pilgrims finally got the opportunity to meet the Indian leader, Massasoit. Massasoit was the sachem (intertribal chief) of all the Wampanoag Indians. He was born in 1590 and died in 1661. He thought there would be peace with the settlers; weren't they wrong? He had shared their planting, fishing, and cooking techniques, which were the key to the settlers' survival in that great new wilderness. Massasoit kept the peace for decades, but more and more of the Europeans came. They arrived with grievous and evil intentions, which created tension to seize land and claim it as their property, and that upset the Indians.

When Massasoit died, goodwill gradually dissolved, leading to the bloody (King Phillip's) War of 1675. The war was led by Massasoit's second son, Metacomet, also known as Metacomet, who adopted the English name King Phillip. The problem with the Indians was that they were shooting with bows and arrows, while the Europeans used guns and cannons. As you study American history, you will see how uneven the battle was for that reason. More Europeans poured into the country, and then things got out of hand. Most of the colonies were formed in the 1600s, and by the 1770s, thirteen British colonies containing 2.5 million people or more populated the country's coastal areas east of the Appalachian Mountains.

After Great Britain defeated France, the British Government imposed new taxes in 1765. The colonists rejected the new taxes, which led to the Boston Tea Party political protest by the Sons of Liberty in 1773. That led to punitive laws by the Parliament designed to end self-government. The Royal Proclamation of 1763, in the Constitution of Canada, stopped Europeans from taking land from the Indians. When they could no longer take it, they would just kill the Indian and remove him from the land.

During the 1800s, they virtually wiped out a race of people from the earth. Slavery was on fire, and the nation was giving birth to a new nation. The creation of a new man, woman, and child instilled within them a twisted mind of deception, something that is instilled in blacks to this very day.

Yes, I said, the new man, the old African spirit, died from the descendants over the years. They endured over 400 years, being stripped, broken down, shredded, ripped apart, and hanged in the darkest hour. They were transported on large ships, packed like sardines in a can. Stacked in layers over the top of each other. When one from the top or above the other peed or messed, it would work its way down upon the other below. They had to smell the rotting flesh and feel the maggots from flies blowing them; they contracted diseases, and many of them died. Their bodies were thrown overboard for the sharks to devour.

Oh, how horrible and miserable this had to be. Some that were sick beyond help were thrown over while still alive for the sharks to rip apart. Was it worth it? To kill and enslave so many people, to live with this as a society, must be a heart-enlarging, mind-decaying experience. Now, one can only begin to understand why, at a certain point in time, you had to wear a wig as a veil to hide behind. With the wig, you were good Sam by day and killer Joe by night without the wig. Only they try to justify the evil it took to build this wicked, made-great nation.

From the formation of the Knights Templars and the exploration of their influence on the rest of the world, it is evident that a religious theology would be the great forgiveness clause to further hide and claim the remission of the greatest sin. The legal owner of slaves taught for over 250 years that a Black man was less than a man. And taught him the inability to love by constantly selling off their companions. This kept his heart unstable and unconditioned for compassion. The black man was a lot like Adam, lonely in the mind. Just like Adam, being separated from the Garden.

Where is the true Black American soul? Is it lost amongst time somewhere? In spite of harshness, the Black man found a way to hide his pain from the captivity of being a slave. He stuck to his religious traits, something in him, a built-in part of his soul; he could not cherish the feeling of vengeance against those he hated the most, deep down within his being. Therefore, he learned to hide and cope with his own personality being suppressed every day of his life, from sunup to sundown. Yes, even with all the darkness, the brightness of the cross of Christ shined, - a better day was coming. The Black American soul suffered from labor all day and sang sacred songs all night to relieve the pain of being enslaved.

Father, I stretch my hands to thee,
no other help I know....

The entrapment of the mind, where one man with a whip could be the overseer and control a massive number of slaves, was established through cruelty and a systemic system of unified law, laws of ownership, and the right to the possession of said property as part of a legal network. Black people do not stick together the way they should; instead, they seem to betray each other for the white man. It appears that the white man has established himself in the minds of some that he reigns in power, thus making himself superior. The first thing that had to happen was to kill the spirit of freedom from the heart and mind of the Black male.

BREAK-DOWN

This breakdown occurred over some time, like over 400 years, the making and breaking as a child being born. Removal of the child from its biological mother to train in a new method of speech stripped the child of its original language, Swahili. This created a communication gap, meaning that the slaves could not communicate with each other, creating a silent moment that lasted more than 200 years. How else could we, as black people, lose our original language completely? It just disappeared from the face of the earth among African Americans. The African Americans were only trained to speak broken Latin without the use of the letter R. To say yes, sir, they automatically would say "yessum"; come here would be "come mea".

They were being set up like livestock, as breeding objects like cattle, goats, sheep, and dogs. Then, they were documented as 3/5th of a human being, not even a whole person. Being fearful of black people becoming like him, the colonists hid the power by suppressing the mind with physical harm. They killed out the original soul of the black being, causing failure inside the mind of a real human being, making them feel less than human and more so, like animals. As this was being done, it deformed the mind psychologically into being an intelligent form of a pet, part man and part beast, with a forgiving heart, regardless of the pain.

When it came to pain, the Africans would not show any emotions from it. Cut off their limbs, pull their teeth, and stick nails through their hands. The Africans would not flinch, even though they felt the pain. This was the only tool they had left other than God. He had to suppress the pain regardless of physical treatment. To eat, he had to kill his Black Brother in fist-fighting and other combat-baiting games that were utilized by his master as entertainment and sports just for pleasure. Most of the by-matches were to the death. A slave lost by being beaten until dead. Thus, he fought like a vicious animal, trying to please his master.

Yes, slavery was Hell brought to life for the Black man. It's hard and unfair. Stop it, I say! The truth is the light. Freedom came to the enslaved people, but no rights.

Abraham Lincoln was killed in this era. When freedom came, people were freed, just to wander about with no place to call home. The women were used as breeding objects and were their masters' chief investment for reproductive purposes. After being freed, they had no sanitation.

Once of no use they were discarded...
Can you say...Cash money?

There were several breeding states and the creation of match-making. This created the ultimate field worker: big, husky, black, and strong. The creation of a new man in the new land.

Character formation of some that were yet to come- the blacker the creation, the more one could tolerate the sun's rays. A dark object absorbs light, and a lighter object reflects, causing it to heat up. Blacks were considered heat tolerators. They had to sleep under trees in the woods. When it would rain, they would be soaked and then dried by their own body heat.

God knows how many died from pneumonia. Now, as I look back over time, I can physically see just how far we have come as a people. There are some in the world today who want to turn the hands of time back from 2019 to the early 19th century.

Take the 1920s, the era when black people had no rights. It's hardcore, but it's true. Much like the 45th and 47th presidents of the United States, Donald Trump, by being careless and reckless with words, expressed his true feelings about the people of color. This nation will never return to those days of old. Because we had people like Joe Biden, who defeated Donald Trump and became the 46th President of the United States.

Biden became President during a time when the worldwide crisis and the pandemic was in full swing, while the scientific world was experiencing the trauma of trying to create a vaccine to fight off the spread of the virus. Masks were ordered to be worn nationwide until the vaccines were developed. People began to get vaccinated on a global scale, but the virus was still killing.

There were new strains of the virus that were mutating and were deadlier than the first. It looked like humanity was being monitored by some invisible force, because when they developed a vaccine to combat the virus, it would mutate, and the new strain would spread to those who had received the first shot.

During this same time, as all of this was unfolding, the President issued a stimulus plan to all Americans to prevent the economy from failing. Several rounds of stimulus checks were implemented in various forms. It took all this to combat the price hack in materials. Lumber and steel went up over 200%, and fuel prices bumped up a small percentage. With everything going haywire and chaos in society, people gunning people down, and race riots stemming from police brutality, historic verdicts came forth from some of the police trials. The killer of Mr. George Floyd got

22 years in Federal prison. We, the people, are still a powerful set of words because they represent the will and pleasure of the people, by a democratic democracy, a free society.

Here we stand, glancing at the impiety of the mind of a man as it's reflected through his actions -discriminating with extreme persistence and prejudice. But we, as black people, are still non-violent; when will that ever end? As a people, we need to test the waters by not being the pets of a harsh society. We are just trapped in the bubble. To be trapped in the bubble is like being incarcerated by time and the turbulence of actuality. Being trapped in this bubble, you can see the outside world clearly, but you can't escape its harsh reality.

We know for a fact that God is on our side; how could we make it this far without him? Because without him, we could do nothing. He freed us from the chains of slavery and set us on a course to escalate beyond the dirt ground level of society. We had an edge. But the bloody, inhumane massacres took place on a people without any physical form of weapons to fight with.

All black people had to fight with was the word of God and their hands, no weapons, like guns, nor a bow and arrow. They were vulnerable and prime victims for lynchings, for battling men with the edge of unity, power, number, and legality, all this on their side, against the people they classified as less than 3/5th of a human being.

Just imagine the effect that alone had on a race of people, being treated less than human, treated as if they were some kind of intelligent pet. This went on for years; blacks were born into this type of environment to have eyes but can't see, have ears but can't hear, have a heart but can't feel, have a mind but can't think, have a God, and be scared to pray. It's from there that we emerged into a broke society with no economic power.

We were taught not to unify under any circumstances but to stand alone and be an island. That is the mentality we developed from. This vital, irresponsible act of treason to humanity-being classified as less than human. Therefore, we betrayed one another by robbing, stealing, and killing each other for a little of nothing.

It makes you wonder
what is the reason for the
treason among black people?

It can only be how the mind has been programmed to survive under harsh conditions- being dependent upon a master for over 400 years. It is a shame that people today don't investigate this factor when it comes to social behavior. The scholars of psychology of this society don't publicize the facts of their true prognosis of what ails society when it comes to the Black race. Instead, they diagnose the children with drugs that will associate them with having a mental disorder. Something that will scar them for the rest of their lives, especially when they get a college education and pursue a government job or a CEO position with a major firm. Then, these reflections on their health become a hindrance.

In the midst of all this are the moral values of how to function as a married couple seeking the American dream in the pursuit of happiness. To have and raise a family and, at the same time, be somebody in life by having access to the world that secures futures for you and the ones you love. But what the majority of black people face is access denied. Now, the silent frustration of disappointment leads to physical, and verbal abuse; then lives fall apart.

Sometimes the male turns to drugs, and the female tries to hold the family together; she is compelled, driven by the forces against her, such as watching the children go lacking for food and other necessities. Put the male on child support; he fails to pay, goes to jail for not being able to pay, unless he sells drugs or commits crimes to support the binding obligation. When he goes to jail for the 5th time, he will be charged as a habitual criminal, and he becomes a felon. Now, the question is, who will hire the felon, regardless of their educational background? Just look at this picture, if you will, on how distorted it is when Black Lives Matter.

All this stems from the past, and America is not letting go; it's getting worse day by day. The black religious community needs to form a hive like the bees. Inside the hive is a leader, which is the Queen; everything works for the benefit of the hive under the authority of the Queen. There are workers of the hive that go out into the field and gather pollen on their legs, fly for miles, and return to the hive, where it is stored in cones built by the cone builders. They even have watchmen of the hive that stand on guard, watching over the hive. Yes, black people need to form the hive. Now, let us look through the telescope of time and focus on an individual's life.

This story I'm about to tell is about a young black man in the South, raised against the odds, fighting for justice and equality by the law, even though he had no more than a first-grade education. His name was Bud Wright, also known as Alex Wright. I talk about Bud in my book, Chicken Scratch. Now, I'm about to reveal the parts that I did not mention.

Bud was born in 1919, just before the Roaring '20s; he also lived through the Great Depression and survived. He was a ten-year-old when the Depression hit. It especially willed hell on black men; the reason- because they didn't have anything anyway. They had less than anyone else.

The Depression hit in 1929 and lasted until 1939. Bud was ten years old when it started and he was around 19 when it ended. When Bud was 11 years old, there was a time at a store. A white boy around the same age as Bud started calling him real nasty names, like darkie, nigger, smut baby, and statements like, You are the blackest nigger I've ever seen.

Well, Bud just left the store, went down the road a ways, hid in the bushes, and waited for the boy to come along. When the young man got to the area where Bud was, Bud jumped out in front of the boy and said It's just you and me now; talk the stuff you were talking about in the store. Bud took his slingshot, loaded it, and aimed it at the boy's face, with the slingshot pulled back as far as he could pull it. The boy turned to run, and Bud hit him in the back of the head; the boy fell to the ground with blood gushing out as if a main artery was cut.

Bud didn't really realize the impact of what he had done, especially leaving the boy for dead. Just so happened that someone came along and found the young man lying in a pool of blood, took the time to see about him, and found that he was still alive. The father was contacted and met up at the doctor's office; the boy was bandaged up, and then the young boy told his daddy what happened and where he was. Bud went on home, and he did not tell anyone what he had done.

The boy's father started investigating. He went to the store, and the storekeeper told him that one of Bish's boys was in the store, and there were some things said. That prompted anger in the boy's father; for someone to almost kill his son and left him to bleed to death on a lonely dirt road. The man rounded up an angry mob and headed for the Wrights' place, carloads of them.

Bud's mother and father were sitting on the porch of their home when they heard the roaring of automobiles heading their way. Not knowing these people were coming to their house. When they rolled up to the yard, the father jumped out of his car and asked for Bishop Wright, saying that he needed to talk to him about an incident that happened earlier in the day. He wanted to know if any of his boys were at the store because he believed one of them hurt his son and left him for dead.

Then the young boy spotted Bud and said, "There he is; that's the one right there that hit me."

Bud came from around the house and said, "I hit him."

"He's a real hothead," the man said, and demanded that he was going to take Bud and teach him a lesson.

Ma Chanie was standing at the door with a double-barreled shotgun. "Nobody is going to take my boy."

Guns appeared from everywhere; Bishop told Ma Chanie to shut up, that he was handling everything, and for her to put the gun down. She said hell would freeze over before she let them take her child anywhere. He managed to get her calmed down and put the gun down. Then he told the man that he was going to whip Bud right then and there. So, he called out to Bud, and Bud came. He told him to look at what he had done.

"We all in danger. Lay down on the ground."

He put his foot on Bud's head and started to beat him, I mean, beat him like he was beating a wild animal. Bud looked the man in the eye while his father was beating him; not one tear fell from Bud's eyes. Bishop continued to beat Bud until the man told him to stop; it was enough, but Bishop kept beating Bud. The man said, " I said stop. I mean, don't hit him another lick."

Well, that ended the uproar about the boy being hit by the slingshot. But things could have gone wrong; after all, this is the same county where Mary Turner, who was eight months pregnant when they strung her up by her heel strings, cut her belly open, and the baby fell out onto the ground, then they riddled her body with bullets. The year was 1918, a year before Bud was born, and the First Antioch Missionary Baptist church was in the planning stage to be constructed in 1920. A black church formed under the authority of a white church.

Black people in Lowndes County did not have any authority; they were controlled under white supremacy. This church cannot be found in any of the history books of Black society because the white overseers would not permit it to be so. A time in 1918 when Sidney Johnson was dragged up and down Patterson Street before the black people, then dragged him to the next nearest town, Morven.

These were the days of hatefulness in the river of rage, where every black soul was living on borrowed time in Lowndes County. A time of no rest, a time of everlasting turmoil for the people of color. Colored signs were posted almost everywhere; a black child, for example, at play, could not even go into a white person's yard to retrieve a ball if it accidentally rolled into their yard. The white people would get the ball themselves and return it, and some would keep it and take the ball from the child; it was bad as well as sad.

In the nostrils of these swimmers of time, the stench of hate seems to fill their lungs, which changed their thoughts toward a race that the majority seem to hate and resent without a cause. The only thing within reason was the color of their skin, thus identifying them as the recipients of almost free labor. The bottom rail Bud was on- he was drowning in the sea of a turbulent time. It was making him, molding him, creating within him a vile, vengeful heart from the harshness of the river of time.

Bud did not realize how close death was upon him and his little family; his father was beating him from that fear. As Bud grew, he truly began to recognize that there was an invisible line of race that he dared not cross. Bud was to understand that during this era of time, he did not have any civil rights. The only rights he seemed to have was to be content with staying on the bottom and living without any hope of succeeding.

He would work along with his parents in the fields from sunup to sundown, never getting the opportunity to go to school, only working and making the white man's money. They received a place to live on the plantation or farm and got a very low income. They had a cow or two, some pigs, chickens, and goats; that was what they would survive on. They knew how to farm and raise crops for the white farmers.

Those that sharecropped had no marketplace that would accept their products. Therefore, they had to sell through the white man, and they could not read or write. They were constantly being taken advantage of by the brokers, who were all white. If they didn't sell through a white person, this included the black people who had their own farms and land. There was no marketplace for the black farmer; they were like a rejected species. A dead-end road was the only future for black people. It seems like freedom was the oppression of the South. What a time this was, merging farther into the darkness of an unknown fate.

Men's and women's hands bore the scars of the cotton bo, hands roughened by touch from toiling under a blistering sun. All this frustration of humiliation was building up in Bud as he grew older; he took after his mother, who was fearless and bold. Hate and a don't give a durn spirit had set in on Bud; it was either do it or die.

Bud's father was a Bishop, teaching him that a man was a man and that all men were created equal. He was more easygoing than his wife. She believed an eye for an eye, tooth for tooth, kill or die, trying to live. She taught all her children to stand their ground, with a kill-or-be-killed attitude, just don't take any mess from any man. Well, all the hate she had went into her children; it definitely went into Bud, plus some. Bud and TB, of the 32 children she had, were deadly. Ten of them had died or been killed before Bud was born. That left twenty-two alive with Bud; he was now old enough to go out and find him a job off the farm.

When Bud turned 17, he went to work at the dairy in the feed room. Where his uncle was the boss. One Monday morning, while at work, his uncle told him to carry one bag of feed into the storage room at the time. Bud refused and started to curse his uncle out, letting him know that he was going to keep taking two bags at a time, one 100-pound bag under each arm. His uncle started to curse back at Bud and told him that he was going to whip him if he didn't act right. At that time, Bud's first cousin heard how he was talking to his dad; so, he ran into the room to take up for his dad, who had just left the feed room. Bud reached over to grab his 12-gauge shotgun, and the boy turned to run. Bang! Bud let him have it; he blew all the seat out of his pants. His uncle came running and saw his son on the ground. Yelling, "Bud shot me, Bud shot me!"

He runs into where Bud is, and Bud points the gun toward him and fires it, hitting him in the same place and blowing the seat out of his pants as well. Now they were both on the ground, yelling, when the boss man came running to see what all the commotion was about. They both were yelling Bud shot me, Bud shot me. The boss went in to see Bud and asked him what happened. Bud kept working and said, "They came in here messing with me, and I shot them in the butt; that's what happened."

He acted as if that was part of the day's labor, just something to do, with no remorse. This is the kind of a man, or real black-at-heart gangster; Bud becomes a part of the turbulent current of this raging river of time.

Well, two years passed, and Bud grew up and got married on August 19, 1938, during the Depression, a time of real hardships. He married Miss Ellaphea Lizimore. She was born August 19, 1916, a very beautiful black woman, dark chocolate in color. She was about two years old when Mary Turner and Sidney Johnson were killed by an angry mob.

She was 21, and Bud was 19 when they got married. She was already dating a young man when Bud took an interest in her. He just walked up to the young man and told him to take a walk, saying she was his woman. Ella was a virgin and had not had any form of a relationship with a man. Well, she ended up with Bud. They had their first child, which was a little girl, and they named her Mary.

Her father was a rigorous man. He was respected by the community and white people as well, for his status as a 33rd-degree Mason, but not as a black man. They respected the fraternity and not the man to a certain degree; he was still Black. The fraternity is built around the philosophy of King Solomon, a black man. One that says I am Black but comely. It just goes to show how the river of time keeps flowing, regardless of theology and all its concepts.

It was already hard times, now a depression. Stepping across the hardships of the time were only steps for a mountain climber. The black man has been scaling this mountain ever since he arrived in this place.

Blacks had no rights during this period. They were just here in the Deep South, in the third most racist state in the union. Racketeering was a way of survival for many blacks, and working as sharecroppers, Bud was both. He was a very dangerous young man; he was a good person, but meaner than a junkyard dog; he was the new black man who could not be broken, as many blacks were.

Conformity was not one of Bud's traits when it came to dealing with the rule of lawlessness against black people in the South. This created some of the most heartless and cruel-minded black men, men who just did not give a darn when it came to the feelings toward a white man. Bud was one of these people. His word was I'll bust a cap. He was the after-effect of cruelty; he was straight-minded when it came to family; it wasn't just white people; it was anyone who rubbed him the wrong way.

When it came to the family, he set the example of what a man is, compassionate with them and other family members, but of course, everyone knew how he was. They knew not to upset him in the wrong way by doing things that were against others, that would be pleasing or appear to be amusing to entertain white people. He hated that; he said that a man was just a man and, in fact, he was a man, not a child. Bud believed in working and trying to have something in life, despite the conditions of the times, fighting against the odds of tradition, a real black man in the notorious true South. Bud worked with bootleggers while he worked as a sharecropper farmer. He hustled moonshine at night and worked the fields during the day.

The only thing was that Bud would not allow his wife or his little girl to work in any field anywhere at all! Of course, that meant problems for Bud. One day, the owner of the farm came to Bud's house and called for him to have his little family come to the field and work.

The farmer said, "Bud, tell Ella and your girl to let's go this morning. Come on, let's go."

Bud's response was, "Let's go where? Where is your wife?"

"She's home," replied the farmer.

"Well, that's where my wife is, and that's where she goner stay." Bud continued, "Where is your daughter?"

The farmer said in school.

Bud said, "That's where mine is going today."

The farmer said, "Nigger you got to go, pack your stuff, and get the hell off my place. I mean, get the hell on off the property."

Bud said, "Ella, pack up our stuff now before I kill this cracker this morning."

Sure enough, they packed up and got off the place. Bud moved on to his father-in-law's place in Cherry Creek, the outer skirts of Valdosta. Mr. Charles Lizmore, known as Big Daddy. His wife's name was Monzina Lizmore. She was known as Big Momma. She was a schoolteacher at Mt. Zion. They owned about 800 acres of prime land, which was land or property that slave owners gave to the freed slaves. By giving freed slaves a portion of the land to work or selling them a portion, which was large plots or many acres, allowed the former slave owner to sustain most of their land and property through sharecropping.

There were several black families in the area that received large sums of land for joining properties. The Wrights, Lizmores, Orrs, Stevins, Belches, and the Washingtons owned several thousand acres of land in the Cherry Creek area.

These people struggled to hold onto their property, but they did. Bud's family was not as fortunate as these families were to get something out of the deal of slavery. There was a different type of mentality between the two families; one had the attitude of ownership, and the other was strictly from the struggle of the South for blacks, being hated because of freedom. It was as if there was a hate freedom act that was legal in the United States of America.

One can imagine the type of scrutiny these families faced just to hold on. These people formed a relationship with one another that could not be broken by any white man. They built their own churches and served God in their own way, promoting freedom as well as prosperity to have independence among men. This type of mentality began and spread throughout Lowndes County and the North Florida area, all the way down to Rosewood, Florida.

Black people of this caliber were serious; they built their empire among themselves, and they had to depend on one another. It was the only help they had- one another. Valdosta, Georgia, for example, had become a thriving City for blacks on the south side of the railroad tracks. This was a time of progression. They even had a Black Chamber of Commerce on the south side. Black businesses were doing very well. There were several dry cleaners, restaurants, pharmaceutical companies, taxicab companies, a BBQ pit, laundry mates, grocery stores, motels, and 100-year-old Churches in the area.

Yes, this was a thriving section of the city of Valdosta. During the early years of segregation, the black community of Valdosta was doing as well as the traditional white community. The Black section of the city was the area designated for blacks to live because of segregation. Yes, like Tulsa, Oklahoma, the place was destroyed, not just by bombings but by the footprint of a bridge.

Being held down as a society, beaten with intent. The way it always seems to be for black people, especially when they are praying for some type of change to come. This was occurring despite the drastic changes within the Government of America. Black men were being elevated in high-ranking offices in many Southern States during the great transition after slavery, when the 44th et seq 10 government was placing Blacks in political power to bring real change to a nation. This didn't seem to have any effect on the deep south Valdosta southern mentality. In Valdosta, things stayed the same. They closed the window of time and let all the rules of civil law pass them by.

This nation was changing or attempting to change by placing Blacks into high positions across America as noted in the *Progress of a race; or, The remarkable advancement of the colored American* published and created by Naperville, Ill., J. L. Nichols & company in 1912. There were black senators and congress members from 1875 to 1881; Bruce B.K. served six years in Mississippi. Revells Hiram served from February 23, 1870, to March 3, 1871, in the State of Mississippi.

In the House of Representatives of Congress, 20 members were elected.

These are those members Cain Richard H. 43d and 45th, 4 years, South Carolina,

Cheatham H.P. 52d and 53rd 4 years in North Carolina, De Large Robt. C 42d 2 years in South Carolina,

Elliott Robt. B. 42d 2 years South Carolina, Haralson Jerry 44th 2 years in Alabama,

Hyman John 44th 2 years North Carolina, Langston John M. 51st 2 years Virginia,

Long Jeff 41st 2 years Georgia, Lynch John R 43d,44th, and 47th 6 years Mississippi,

Miller Thos. H 51st 2 years South Carolina, Murray Geo. W. 43d and 54th, 4 years, South Carolina,

Nash Chas. E 44th 2 years Louisiana, O'Hara Jas.E. 48th and 49th 4 years North Carolina,

Rainy Jos. H 44th et seq 10 years South Carolina, Ransier A J 43d 2 years South Carolina,

Rapier Jas. T 43d 2 years Alabama, Smalls Robt.S. 44th , 45th, and 47th 6 years South Carolina,

Turner, Benj. S. 42d 2 years Alabama, Wall Josiah T. 42d, 43d, and 44th 6 years Florida, and White Geo.H. 55th 4 years North Carolina.

These were the times when America was preparing for dramatic changes, and it was happening under President McKinley.

In 1901, the President appointed Blacks to high offices, such as Collectors of Customs; nine were selected. Naval officers 2 were selected, Ministers plenipotentiary 3 were selected, and the Secretary of Legation 1 was selected. There were 13 others, including 5 Army surgeons.

These were the years and time frame during which the stages for change were set. Even though America was rebelling subconsciously from deep within her bowels.

Bud was caught up in the reactor of time, trying to transcend by being a blue-collar worker.

He had learned to farm from the way of life in the South; just being black was a farming curse, and he worked the fields. This was the path Bud would have to tread as he plodded through the

* * *

journey of time, he and his little family, as they moved from place to place. Looking for a home was difficult for him because he would not allow his wife or children to work outside the home.

———————◆———————

As a few years had passed, they had another child, a son. Ella named him Charles, with a nickname—Sonny. Sonny grew up to be a guy who really didn't care about much. He took one of Bud's blue surd suits and waded out into a pond to muddy it up so that the fish would come to the top of the water, so that he could catch them.

Sonny would shack up with women for a few years, then he would tell them that he was going to the store to get a loaf of bread, and he would keep going, and they wouldn't see him for a few years. But when he came back, he'd bring a loaf of bread. I just had to mention that.

Well, Bud was the kind of young man who loved the fast life and women, but kept his home intact. It was hard for a Black man in general; it seemed as if he had to be willing to love while being filled with hate.He had to learn how to have a family and struggle with reason, because all the reasons were against him.

Therefore, men like Bud were the product and fabric of the twisted society, men and women without rights. This was a re-minder to Bud of his childhood, when his father beat him for the incident with the little white boy. To be held down by the foot of his father on his head, he knows the feeling of paying the price by being the victim.

There was a time Bud went out just to have a good time, drinking shine, while making a few dollars bootlegging. He and his brother, T.B., were out in the woods in Moultrie, GA, at a juke joint built from a hulled-out house where the room walls were removed to allow more space for gambling and dancing.

Bud and a young lady were dancing, and while they were dancing, a man accidentally stepped on Bud's foot. Bud told the man that he had stepped on his foot, and the man replied to Bud.

He said, 'Your mouth is big enough; put your foot in it.' Bud stopped dancing, turned to the man, and shot him several times, at close range, and it set the man's clothes on fire.

That night, Bud had worn T B's army uniform, and the people thought Bud was T B, because they looked so much alike. Everyone said T-B had just shot a man, and the joint emptied out; the partying ended for the night. T.B., being in the army, made his way back to the place where he was stationed. Bud went back home as if nothing had happened; the law was looking for T.B., not Bud. Bud was asked a few questions, but not many; the law really didn't care as long as it was a Black killing a Black.

Blacks were just Trapped In The Bubble.

Well, Sunday came, and they had the funeral at Mount Olive Baptist Church, and Bud went to the service. The man had six brothers; they looked back into the audience and spotted Bud in the back section of seats.

One said this man, done killed my brother, and come to his funeral. Then all six jumped on Bud, he pulled out a 38 revolver, and began to shoot in the church. All the brothers and the people jammed the door, pouring out of the church.

Someone got the law out there. Bud had gone into a cornfield by the time the law came. The word got around to Big Daddy, Bud's father-in-law, one of the prominent black men in the area. The law would at least listen to him for a little while. Big Daddy knew the law would kill Bud without hesitation, and they said to Big Daddy, "You know we will have to kill this one; we've heard of him."

So Big Daddy pleaded with them to let him go into the cornfield and try to persuade Bud to turn himself in. Big Daddy called Bud's name as he walked through the corn field, continuously talking, telling him not to make his daughter a widow.

"These red necks are going to kill you today, Bud, so son, please come with me, they are going to take you to jail, and that's it, nobody got hurt back there at the church."

Then Bud spoke up, "I will let the air out your big butt, too."

"If they hear a shot, they coming in and kill us both, so give me the gun and let's go, my boy. Come on, let's go," Big Daddy said. Bud humbled himself and went with his father-in-law, and they grabbed Bud and took him to jail.

Well, that Monday came, and Bud didn't show up at the farm for work. The farmer went to the jail and said, 'I heard you got my boy down here, and I came to pay his bond. Let him go, and I mean now.' When Bud got out, the farmer told him, 'You stay out of hell; I'll keep you out of jail.' It wasn't long after that things cooled down and went back to normal.

Bud would work every day on the farm, planting fields; tractors weren't popular in the area. Bud would use a team of two mules to plow with. Bud said he fed them so good you could hear them fart two hundred yards away.

James Wright and Bud, along with their brothers Leroy and Cal Wright, would help gather tobacco. David Wright, one of Bud's older brothers, had a bad foot due to a birth defect. As a result, he was a very hateful person and would kill you if you laughed at his condition. However, he was a valuable help on the farm when he was around. *They be done* worked hard and couldn't hardly wait for Friday evening to go jitterbugging. That was a dance called the jitterbug.

They had three sisters alive with them: Odessa Wright, Sage Wright, and another named Mildred Wright, known as Millie. Boy, they say she could dance, both ways, clean, and nasty. They would clown around and drink that shine all night long, playing poker, rolling them dice, and letting the good times roll.

These were dangerous times,
people, and places; somebody
would get cut from time to time.

Some of the farms Bud worked on were two, three square miles. If not square, they would be ½ mile wide and several miles long. It was very easy to find a farm that was a 1000 acres plus.

Yes, these were the times when Black people stuck together, yet there were some of them that had inherited trait; showing ignorance by being ignorant in the worst way, being the showroom clown; act silly or pick fights, curse at people for no reason, just to get attention, be the center of attention, what do you say about that?

Late one evening, everyone was having a joyful day, and the movie *Gone With the Wind* was playing at the drive-in theater. Black people were not allowed inside the parking lot or on the drive-in premises. They had to park along the roadside, and watch the movie from their vehicles, or sit on the curbside between trees, or wherever they could find an opening in the trees or brush.

Anyway, Mama Ella and Bud's sister, Millie, said that they were going to the movies. Bud told Mama Ella that she could not go and for her to stay home. Well, she insisted that she was going and was determined she would go. Well, Bud went in and got his shotgun, loaded it with bird shots. Millie went to Mama Ella, put her arms around her, and said to Bud, "If you shoot her, you got to shoot me too."

Bud raised his gun and shot them both around their legs. They broke and ran into a cornfield. Bud yells, "Now you gone with the wind." They were not hit by very many of the bird shots, just enough for them to know he meant business, and he was Bud Wright. They would make up, and everything worked out well between them all.

They were just that kind of a family.

Black people had merged from not knowing how to show love, because of the social disconnect in the humane prospect of life. They related to each other from the heart and showed love in many different ways. Some women said that their husbands did not love them if he didn't beat them physically.

What kind of a mind is that for a person to have, the slave master trait? That's like being brainwashed to the most extreme degree. Have someone beat them and call it love; that is a deformed and distorted mind. The concept of the fact that slavery's harshness created this twisted metaphor in the minds of the oppressed.

One Saturday night late spring, downtown in a juke joint owned by a white man for black people, whites would very seldom go into the juke for that reason. There was this great social divide between the races, Black and White. Even though it was a social divide, a few white people used it to their advantage to get rich by owning a place like that, an integrated bar, that no whites would attend unless they were dangerous or the law.

Well, that evening or night, a black man from the railroad came into the juke joint. And started to take over the place. A man and his wife would be dancing, and this guy would just walk up and be very disrespectful to the couple. He would grab the woman and just shove the man down to the floor, talking trash the entire time. Saying things like *get up, you sorry son of A, before I put my foot in your -*, then start kicking the man before he could get up from the floor.

Boy, was this guy bad news. He'd then leave this couple and start on another by touching a lady inappropriately. Her boyfriend would try to stand up for her, and the guy would just grab the young man, slap him around, and throw him down to the floor. Then he'd say, " I don't allow nobody to stay in a joint while I drink, everybody out."

So the people got up and started walking out just to avoid this guy and getting into any trouble. By this man working for the railroad, he had probably been getting away with this kind of stuff for a while in other places.

Well, everyone except a few left out of the juke, among the few set Bud at the bar. The man walks up to Bud while he was taking a drink, leans over and gets close to Bud's ear, and yelled, "Boy, perhaps you didn't hear me, get your black butt up, hit the dam door now!"

Bud pushed away from the bar a little, kind of leaned back. "Are you talking to me, or are you sho, you talking to Mr. Alex?"

The man said, "You dam right I don't know about no Mr. who, but I'm talking to you."

"Is that right?" Bud said. Then he got up like he was leaving, like everyone else. The only thing was that Bud went *to go* out another way, the back door, which had a two-by-four about three and a half feet long as a brace across the door for a lock of some kind. Bud reached and grabbed the board from the door, then eased in and tipped up behind the man.

Boy Bud let him have it right beside the head; the man's jaw teeth flew out the front of his mouth. Then Bud kicked him in the seat of his pants and took the board and beat his pants off of him, then the man found his way out of the juke, with his rear kicked. That was the last time he was ever seen in Valdosta.

The owner told Bud, 'I don't know why all the people got up and walked out, because this is my place.' The reason I didn't say anything is that I knew he would eventually get around to you. Then Bud stayed, finished his drink, and left for the night.

———◆———

Sundays was always a religious day among Black people-until late evening for some. They end up sitting on their porches, looking down the road for who's coming. Sometimes they would have fish fry's. If so, all those from around the countryside who had heard about the fish cooking would come. They were the same way when they heard something had gone wrong for one of them. They would have what was known as a big meeting.

That was when everybody Black would hear of a problem, and come together regardless of their denomination. There was a unity among them that was hard to be broken. There was this un-explainable beauty and love cultivated by hate, from the hidden fear of being victimized at any time, for no reason. They could die for stealing a chicken, or just be caught off alone, and be a victim of drunks, who just spotted them, a person alone, and hang him or her just for fun. These were the days without civil rights, and it created some very hard-core men.

One day, Bud, Millie, and Leroy were cruising through town, and they looked and saw one of their cousins standing, watching, as two white men attacked his wife.

The cousin allowed one of the men to rip his wife's blouse off, and he did absolutely nothing.

Leroy said, "Did y'all see that?"

Mildred said, "I saw it."

Bud said, "I see'd that. When we get to the corner, I'm going to pull over to the curve and park. Leroy, you drive and keep the car running. Mildred, I want you to walk in front of me. Here they come."

The two men came walking toward Bud and them. Bud told Mildred, When I say step aside, you just step to the side and get out of the way. Well, when the men were just about to them, Bud told Millie to step aside; she did so. Bud hit one of the men so hard that when the other man saw his partner hit the ground the way he did, and the way Bud was stomping and beating the guy, he broke and ran. He left the scene yelling that there's a big black, killing my friend, help, he's killing him.

Bud jumped in the car and told Leroy to take him to the country. When they got to the woods, he changed clothes and went right back into town. When he arrived, the police were talking to the man Bud had beaten.

Bud, with cold nerves, walked up to the guy, put his hand on the man's shoulder, and said Great God, man, what on earth happened to you. The man said it was a great big, black boy that done this to me. And the man kept talking to the police, and never identified Bud as the assailant. Bud got away with that, and he went on about his business.

Bud worked around farming and started dairying as a part-time job. He would wear a Dobbs hat all the time when he would go out, he love his Blue surd suit, a floor shine shoes, and drove no other car, than a Cadillac. He turned into class. In other words, Bud was a classy guy, for a black man or gangster. Bud found out who he was and that he wanted something out of life. He wanted ownership and money. Bud knew that was power and the nearest thing to true freedom.

One morning, Bud was out and about driving around, done had a few drinks of shine, and he decided to see how fast his caddy would run. He hit a curve and lost control. He had a terrible accident; he was thrown from the car, and his head plowed into the ground. When the officials arrived, they found him wandering around with his 38 in his hand.

They asked him what he was doing, and he said he was hunting rabbits. Then he passed out. They rushed him to the hospital, there they drilled three quarter-size holes in the top of his head to relieve the pressure from bleeding. Bud had a rough and rugged road ahead to recover. The family stood by him, with Big Daddy and Big Momma helping to keep his family going, along with his parents, Ma Channy, and Bishop Alex Wright.

After he recovered, he was supposed to have steel plates put in his head where the quarter-size holes were drilled in his head, but it never happened. He would not even go back to the doctors, but he had problems; he would have these terrible headaches, to the point he could hardly sleep. When Momma Ella would play the radio, he would take his gun and shoot it, even the TV. When he would drive, he drove real slow; he was on the edge of nutting up.

But by the Grace of God, he was able to overcome the trauma, but it still left a bad scar on his mind. When he got angry, he was worse than he was before; he would lose it, but always stuck to his guns.

He reached a point where his mind was almost back to normal, and he learned to cope with things. When he got up, he went to work for Mr. Sheffield, another prominent farmer. Bud worked for him for a year or two, then he was persuaded to try another farmer in the area. Then Bud and Ella's daughter, Pricilla, was born.

He still knew farming, and he was good at dairying, so he moved to a farm with a farmer who wanted him as a sharecropper.

Well, everything was going rather well for Bud, so he thought. He had 50 acres of his own land to farm, to take care of his family. Bud felt as if he was in what you call high cotton; the only thing was, he was about to go for the ride of his life, by not having an education.

Bud would not allow his wife to have anything to do with what he called man's business. His wife's mother was a schoolteacher; therefore, she taught her daughter, Ellaphea, very well. Ella was really good with numbers and could read extraordinarily well. Even at that, Bud would not allow her to interfere with his work.

They farm the land, planting crops such as cotton, corn, cucumbers, tobacco, watermelons, and a few soybeans. They seem to have the green thumb when it came to farming; they produced strong crops. However, Bud not being able to read at all, the farmer took advantage of the opportunity to beat this man out of his share he produced. When the time came for them to settle, the farmer told Bud, "You just did break even; maybe you will do better next year."

The other black farmers had heard that Bud just broke even, and they talked among themselves. One of Bud's best friends, Mr. Donnale Crawford, told him, "You need to watch that farmer, he a crook when it comes to Black people."

———————————

Mr. Crawford owned hundreds of acres of land, and he was pretty well off and very independent. Well, the following year, Bud worked the farm and had a very good harvest across the board. Then it came time to settle up for the year, and the man came back from the market. He met with Bud and explained that he had done a little better than last year. However, it was still not enough to amount to anything. This was a real setback for Bud.

Big Daddy had heard how Bud and Ella had fared dealing with that farmer. He sat down with Bud and began explaining that perhaps he should allow Ella to help him keep track of all his receipts, so that everything would tally.

Then, later that same day, Bud met with his friend and Elder Shanks, his mentor, and had a serious business talk with them about his situation with the farmer. He told them how Big Daddy had expressed himself, that his daughter would be able to help him if he would permit her to.

They looked at Bud and said to him, "Big Daddy was right; maybe you ought to let her help you."

After a few drinks, Bud went home. When he got there, he told Ella that he was going to let her help him keep up with everything, then he lay down and went to sleep. Well, the next day it was time for him to go to work, and Ella asked him a question.

"You know what you said last night?"

"About you helping me," and she said, "Yes, how can I help you?"

Bud said, "By keeping up with everything I use?"

Then Bud told her, 'I don't want you to come to the field, because this man may get the wrong idea. And start wanting you to work, and he is only to deal with me, not you, y'all not going to work in their dam fields, and I mean that.' Ella understood.

"Here's what I need you to do Bud: bring me the label off of every bag, every receipt, anything marked' paid 'with a dollar, and I will keep a record and tally them for you. We will keep track of your harvest the same way, and we will get the going price from Daddy and them who have their own farms. We are set?" They agreed.

Bud went to work and made sure to do what Ella asked him to do. He did this day in and day out until the year passed. Ella had kept up with everything; it was a clear-cut profit. Bud felt really good about how things were going, knowing he was about to get the money he needed to put him in the big leagues, along with Big Daddy, Mr. Crawford, and Mr. Jim Woods. He was really looking for the change in his life in the heat of it all.

The farmer took everything to the market. When he returned to the farm, he drove up to the place not far from the big house, his house, of course. He asked Bud to get in the truck with him. Bud had been working on the fence all day. He had a staple hammer on his side; this hammer is made like a regular hammer on one side, with a sharp, curved hook on the other side. The farmer began to tell Bud how things went at the market.

"Bud, dad nabbit, I don't see how you do it, you did it last year, the year before, turn around and did the same thing this year, dad blame it, you just did jump the fence."

The moment he said that, Bud jumped the fence with the hammer, striking the farmer on the head. The hammer got stuck inside the man's head, but Bud snatched it out. The man managed to stumble out of the truck. Bud ran around to him and struck him again with the claw side in the rib, and the farmer hit the ground.

Bud took the money, which was his, and took the rest and threw it in the man's bloody face. The farmer's wife heard the noise, came out to see the commotion, lo and behold, what she saw was a black man killing her husband. She broke out in a raging, panicking run.

Bud jumped up off the farmer and started after her, but she managed to escape. She jumped a six-foot fence in fear for her life. Bud knew he was done for. He had just beaten this man he thought to death, which meant doom in Lowndes County.

He started to run and went to a man named Melow Stiven. He put Bud in the trunk of his car and took him to Jacksonville, Florida. It didn't take very long; all of Lowndes County was looking for Bud.

Ella and the two children were left alone, although she was badgered by the law. Ella went home to Big Daddy and stayed there for quite some time. Then, after months had passed, she thought that Bud had been taken. She took off with her and the three children and went to Miami, Florida. There, she waited for a while and let months pass; then, one day, she and the children took off for Jacksonville, Florida.

Bud had found a place in Bryceville, Florida, working at a dairy farm under his middle name, Andrew Wright. The man he worked for was Mr. Carter, at Carter's Dairy, as a milkman. Well, Ella and the children soon met up with Bud; weren't they glad to see one another. Ella and Bud were very compassionate with each other. They spent the entire evening alone, planning how they would have to live. Especially for what Bud had done, as far as he knew, he had killed a Big white man in Georgia. And an (A P B) all point bulletin had been issued for his arrest, which meant he really had to lay low for quite some time. He could not be seen in public places where he might be identified.

The fact was that the man did not die; he was still alive, messed up in the head, but alive. He died years later. The thing was, Bud and Ella thought the man was dead, and they lived looking over their shoulder for a few years, Ella would do all the shopping while Bud stayed at home and just worked at the dairy farm.

Carter had come to depend on Bud for everything, but he just couldn't get Bud to go into town. Instead, Bud would find something to do, because it was always work at the barn or around the dairy farm.

Years went by, and Ella had several children: Chester, Vernier Mae Wright, known as Hank Walk; Elizabeth Wright, known as Freddy; Janie Wright, known as Geechee; Caro Wright; Alexis Wright, known as Little Fellow; and Terrie Lynette Wright, known as Papoo.

As the children grew, Bud taught them how to milk cows and how to break down and sanitize the milk machines. He took the boys, not the girls. Ella took the girls, and Bud spoiled them. By giving them everything he could afford to give them within his power. He loved his family and did not mind working to take care of them.

No one can ever say that he did not love or take care of his loved ones. He never mistreated them under any circumstances. He tried to show them the way. Even his daughter, Terrie, had slipped and gotten credit at a store unknown to Ella. It was a small bill, and her sister Pre found out about it and told on her, because Terrie had hidden the items in the bushes. She received two licks for throwing the items away, not because of the credit.

Bud knew she had a credit because the store owner knew him and told him about it. He really spoiled her that way, by letting her have her way mostly; he was the number one dad when it came to her. He was just Bud when it came to anyone else, unless he thought something of the person.

He was just trapped in the bubble.

The Black struggle of existence in this white man's created nest. Unjustifiably built from the blood of many. Broken down within the mind, not the body or its limbs, just the mind that controls the limbs. Because all the body parts are only tools of the mind. Break down the mind, and it controls the body.

For over 300 years, the minds of black men of this nation have been tampered with by inhumane, harsh conditions, mentally and physically. As the years passed, Bud began to venture out from the dairy, going into the black section of town only. Segregation was the norm of the times.

Bud had another son outside of his marriage, about the same age as Chester, named Theodor Wright, known as Theado. Bud was a womanizer; he loved some women. He was a character to deal with; he was just Bud. *As time moved on the past was what it became, the past to Bud.*

Years added up, and time went by like a flash. The children were older. Bud was in his late 30s and early 40s; he quit looking over his shoulders. He became a master craftsman of the Dairy; he could operate it as if it were an extension of himself. He learned to deliver calves and perform surgery on cows, just like a real, licensed veterinarian.

There was a time when a cow could not give birth to a calf, and the certified Veterinarian said the cow was going to die as well if the calf couldn't be removed from the cow. And that he did not have a way of removing the dead calf.

The Vet left the dairy for the cow to die, as there was nothing anyone could do. Then Bud took a single-blade razor, stuck his arm inside the cow, and dissected the dead calf without damaging the cow's insides. As he dissected a part, he would pull it out of the cow; he did this until the dead calf was completely removed, thus saving the cow's life.

———————

Mr. Carter allowed Bud to become the foreman, and he ran the entire dairy's day and night shifts. Carter came to understand the kind of man Bud was. One day, Bud's grocery was low at the house, and times were a little hard and tight. But Bud had a taste for some beef for himself and his family.

Bud took the Jeep from the dairy and went to the back side of the pasture. There, he spotted a big, healthy, stocky beef cow. He took the jeep and ran into the cow, knocking it over. Bud jumped out of the jeep, cut the cow's throat, tied a rope and chain to its legs, and dragged it behind the Jeep.

Now, first of all, Bud doesn't own a cow —especially not beef stock —it belonged to the dairy or Mr. Carter; and Bud did not ask or did he buy; he just jumped in the Jeep and went to the back pasture, where he got himself a cow, and dragged it past Mr. Carter's house. Mr. Carter saw what he did.

Bud took the cow home. Once home, Bud and the family butchered it and carved out steaks and all. Momma Ella went in and cooked fresh steaks for the family, and they rejoiced. The very next day, Mr. Carter approached Bud and said, 'I see you got some beef yesterday.' Bud said, 'You darn right, I got the biggest one I seed'.

Mr. Carter just looked at Bud and shook his head, saying, 'Well, Bud, carry on.' 'I think you got things going pretty well. Keep up the good work.'

On the diary farm Bud would do all the hiring and firing from this point, so he hired his family, whose lives would prove to be very interesting. They were full of adventures; it seemed like one thing after another.

His brother, James Wright, also known as the Big O, would cut a person at the blink of an eye; he was a knife-man. He could open a Barlow type knife as fast as Clint Eastwood could draw his gun from his holster. And on top of it all, The Big O was mean; some say he went for bad, but others say that was just how he was.

Yes, the Big O was a bad man with a knife, until one day there was this little, short white man who worked at the dairy with them, and he was taking a drink with them. It was The Big O's liquor bottle, and The Big O said, 'For nobody to drink directly out of my bottle, please get a glass or jar; just get something, just don't drink from the bottle.'

Well, the man decided that he would drink straight from the bottle. When he did, the Big O jumped him, started beating the little guy, and he could do nothing with Big O (Otis), except take the beating.

He managed to get his hand in his pocket and pulled out a small case knife, which he stuck in the Big O's chest. When the Big "O felt the pain, he jumped up, ripping himself wide open from the top of his chest down to his pelvis.

He ran after the little white man until his guts fell, and he had to grab them to hold them in. They rush The Big O to the hospital, where they sew him up. He carries this scar for life in the memory of the bottle, the glass, and, of course, the little, short, white man.

He stayed out of work for quite some time after that. Bud saw about him and carried him all the way until he recovered, because The Big O was his sister's son, Sage.

Bud also hired both his sons and little James, his brother's son. Little James had a mental problem and was strong. I mean very strong. He would say that his chest was bursting open, and only a Coca-Cola would stop the bursting of his chest. He'd get the cola, drink it, and roar loudly like a lion or some wild beast. He was not always like this; he had been normal before he went to New York.

One time, Little James went to New York City following the racehorses, specifically the racehorse, and a so-called friend of his poisoned his drink, then gave him an overdose of heroin, which messed his mind up for life.

There was a time later in life when he thought he was a vampire; he had to have some blood to drink. He looked at Glory; she was high yellow, close to being white, and she became his target. He began to stalk her, hiding behind buildings, peeping around the edge, watching her.

Poor Aunt Glory had no idea that she was being stalked by little James, on the verge of losing her life. Just as Little James had eased and slipped up on her, raised his hand with a knife to stab her, but Bud so happened to see him, and yelled out his name, James!

Little James broke and ran into a field where there were some cows and young calves. He caught a calf, cut its throat, caught a quart of the calf's blood, and drank it. This incident hit the newspapers about a man drinking cows' blood.

Then, sometime later, about six months after, one morning at a store in the black section of town, Little James was talking loudly and cursing very badly. A man walked up to him and told him not to curse like that in front of his old lady. He began to curse at James, telling him how he just got out of prison, and how he was on his way back if he didn't quit cursing in front of his wife, that he was going to put his foot in his---.

Well, at that time a man that was standing by, said hey mister, I'm not getting into your business, but can I whisper something in your ear? The man said yes, but make it quick, so I can finish with this man. The man leaned over and whispered into the gentleman's ear.

"Do you read the paper? That's the man who cut the cow's throat and drank the blood."

The man immediately turned to James and said, 'That woman hears that kind of stuff all the time. You haven't said anything she hasn't heard before. She's just a woman. You just go ahead, sir, and have a nice day.'

I recall a time when Little James went to work with a man named Turner Gary, the father of the famous attorney Willie Gary, and they cut cabbage in the cabbage field. It had come a real hard rain that soaked the field really good, and it became boggy, and the tractor got stuck with a load of cabbage attached to it. They had other tractors to help, but they could not get them out or unstuck.

Little James said to Mr. Turner, 'I can get it out.' Mr. Turner turns to Little James, 'Son, you cannot get that out; you see, those tractors couldn't get them out.' Little James said, 'I can.'

He gets up and walks over to the back of the trailer, loaded with cabbage. He reached down and grabbed hold of the trailer and started to lift it. His feet sank into the dirt until they went out of sight. Every vein and leader in his arms and neck stood out as he lifted the trailer out of the mud. Once the trailer was clear, he set it over on hard ground.

Everyone was shocked, but Mr. Turner was beyond that; he was scared. He became frightened of Little James, paid him for the whole day, and told him he didn't have to work. I just had to put that in about Little James.

Well, back to the structure of things. Mary had married Earl Shanks, whom Bud had also hired. One Friday morning, Bud was underneath his car, checking the oil drain plug, when the car fell on him; the jack slipped from under the car as it rolled. Earl Shanks reached down and grabbed hold of the car, lifting it up off Bud, where he got the strength to do that, nobody knows. Bud was ok; he had some bruised ribs, but none were broken.

Priscilla married Joe Hamilton, who worked in the pulpwood industry. He was a loader. Joe was built and drank a lot of wine. Joe would fight with everyone when he got too much to drink; other than that, he was a very good, hardworking man.

Vernie Mae married Robert Lincoln Gary the 3rd, who loved wine until he became addicted to it. He was also a migrant worker, a very good man. Carolyn married Bristol, who was also a dairy-man and a very good guy. Later in life, Bristol died after he and Carolyn had separated. She then married a very respectable man named Ike. He is the real deal — a superhuman being who would do anything to help anyone who tried to help themselves. He helped all of Carolyn's children get started in life in the educational field.

The only thing about Ike is that he didn't play; he was, and still is, a very serious person. Papoo (Terrie) - well, she married Doc, the one the story of Chicken Scratch is about. That's the layout of the family.

Uncle James Bud's brother's wife was named Gloria, and she was a high-yellow woman, a pretty one at that. Well, one day, while working at the dairy, this white man would tease James about Gloria. He would say things like, 'James, Gloria must not have given you none last night.' Bud heard the remark and told James, 'Stop him now, or he's going to say worse things than that about you and your wife.' Bud started cursing, telling the man he doesn't play that shit.

Three days later, the man made another wisecrack to James. James just looked down and walked away. Then, the man turned to Bud and said, "Bud, Ella." That's as far as the man got. Bud locked all his fingers around his neck and started choking him. Bud choked him down to the ground, got down on top of him while still choking him.

All the men at the dairy tried to get Bud off the man, but they had to pry Bud's fingers from around the man's neck. The man had changed colors and soiled his pants; Bud choked the mess out of him.

When the man got where he could get up without their help, he wobbled and staggered his way to his car. Bud ran up to him and kicked him as hard as he could in the butt.

The man broke and ran for his life, got in the car in a panic, fumbling with the keys, and looked back to see if Bud was coming. He went to Mr. Carter and told him what had happened. Before he could get the words out, Carter said, "You must have said something to Bud."

"That was the nigger it was," replied the man.

Carter said, "Well, Bud is who I got running things, just can't play with him." Well, the man quit and went to work somewhere else.

———————

Bud and his family would go fishing sometimes, and Bud would go hunting. There was this one time when they muddy the waters. They would wade in the water and stir up the mud, which would cause the fish to come up for air. When they did, they would be grabbed and put into a fish basket.

One day, Bud grabbed a big black moccasin snake. He panicked while holding it by the neck, and when Bud dropped it, the snake was dead, cold dead. Uncle James grabbed an alligator turtle, and it bit off Uncle James's finger. Aunt Glory went to screaming about Uncle James's finger; it was bad, but life went on.

Aunt Glory picked up a boyfriend, and James found out about it. One day, the man came out to the dairy, where the houses were located down the lane. The man came out there in a pickup truck with running boards on the sides. Uncle James ran and jumped on the side and went to whaling the man aside the head. Every time he hit the man, the man would holler, and as his face began to swell, the truck stopped. The man went out the other side and hit the ground running. James couldn't catch him; that ended the boyfriend deal. Then he went home and got on Aunt Glory until she broke camp.

Then, Uncle David told James that the man had been going with Glory, and a man named Mr. Norwood called Dave a liar. Uncle Dave took out a barlow knife and stabbed the man in the heart, killing him. The man went about 75 yards and fell. Meanwhile, Bud and James got the man onto the porch to try to help him, while someone sent for the police and ambulance.

Meanwhile, Uncle Dave went into the kitchen, got some grits, came, and sat down on the man while he ate. Bud told him that he should not do that. Dave said, 'Be still before I kill you again.' When the law arrived, the man had bled to death, and they went to put the cuffs on Bud. Bud yelled out, 'Hell, I didn't kill the man, shucks, my brother did.' So, they took Dave in. Williamena, Dave's old lady, came to see about him, but he was gone already.

Before this happened, Williamena and Dave would fight; he would take his rifle, knock her down, stick the barrel up into her private parts, and say I will blow the bottom out your---. He was the kind of man that, if a fly landed on his hat, which was a Stetson, he would take his shotgun and kill the fly. His roof had all kinds of patches where he had shot holes, shooting at flies for landing on his hat. He went to prison for a few years. During that time, he got cancer in the throat and lungs. He started drinking a lot, and life went on for him and others around them.

Then one day, while he was at Bud's house, he took off running and gasping for breath. His lungs just stopped working; he ran until he could go no farther. He got down on one knee, and his eyes seemed as if they were going to come out of their sockets. Terrie, his niece, saw him. She asked her mother why he was running like that, and she replied that he was running from death. Sure enough, he died on the spot. This was the life that black people like Dave lived, and they didn't seem to care too much about anything, not even people.

———◆———

Strangely, their father was a Bishop in the Church. Bud would have visions, you know, like seeing things that aren't there. He would be driving along, and suddenly stomp on the brakes, and say, 'Great God, do you see that?' Look at the city of pure gold, look yonder y'all, see how it's shining? I know you see that," he says. Then, after everyone convinces him that they don't see anything, he keeps looking, and it goes away. Bud was a very good person; he would give the shoes from his feet and the shirt off his back. He just didn't take anything off anyone.

Coming from the times of hard knocks, a black man in the true south had no rights, and was classified as being 3/5th of a human being; labeled part man and part beast, can the man overcome the beast?

Is that whereas ever he lays his head
can become a home, with no place in mind?

Just be able to create a world from within that he could live in and rise above the line of ignorance, when blacks just kill one another for whatever reason. This is a part of the mentality, that seemingly built-in trait, the ruthless curse of slavery. A man's mind, captured from toiling with the grind, from day in -day out, of the same thing, suppression.

Can you feel it, Trapped in a Bubble.

Bud and his brothers and sisters may have gotten their ways from their mother. She was a very short lady, standing at four feet two or something. She had nerve of steel; they say she blew down the barrel of a double-barreled shotgun that was drawn on her and the bishop. They say it stripped away the power felt by the white man who was holding the weapon when she took hold of both barrels, looked him directly in the eyes, and blew down the barrels.

Then she took the gun and gave it to her husband, and said, "Let a real man take it." Then she pulled up the long dress above her knees and climbed back on the two-horse buggy. Just maybe that's where the nerve of her children came from.

That nerve and determination fueled Bud. He wanted something out of life; he would take calves from the dairy and sell them, hustle shine, gamble with dice, but never cards of any kind.

———————•———————

Well, as time passed, Dave got out of prison due in part to the fact that he was ill with a terminal cancer. One night, Dave, Bud, and a few other men were rolling dice. One of the men lost a large amount of money in the game. Dave had eased some crooked dice into the game, and the man found out about them by grabbing the dice. Examining the dice, they were loaded and would most likely fall on the heaviest side.

The man played it off as if he hadn't noticed the dice were loaded; he played a few more rounds, got up, and left. Soon, he came back with a single-barrel 12-gauge shotgun.

When the man raised the gun to shoot Dave, Bud pushed the door close against the barrel, the man snatched the gun from the door, and the door closed. The man shot through the door and hit Bud in the thigh; pieces of wood, along with shots, were in his leg. Bud went home, and Ella met him at the door, giving him his gun.

When Bud got back, the man was gone, and from there he went back to Ella, then to the hospital. The doctor took a large scoop scalpel, and just removed the mutilated muscle that the shotgun had damaged.

It took time for Bud to heal; Uncle James, Earl Shanks, and the rest of the family took care of them and kept the dairy going. Eventually, Bud got to the point where he could stand on the leg, but he wanted to get back to work. He did light-duty work until he healed.

CHAPTER

4

Well, eventually Bud did heal, and he wanted revenge, so he went where the man who shot him hung out and just stalked him. Bud watched him as he drank until the man was drunk. The man got so drunk that he passed out, and when he did, Bud moved in, picked up the guy, and loaded him inside of his car. Bud took him to a remote area where there was a railroad track and laid him on the track, and left him there to die from the train.

But as he drove off and got down the road, it came to him that the man was not after him, but after his brother, Dave. Then he drove off a little way and stopped in the middle of the road, turned around, and went back to get the man off the tracks. Bud took the man home. He picked him up and carried him to his house.

A lady who knew Bud and how he was said, "I just don't believe what I see." She asked Bud, "Is that you?" Bud answered and said, "Yes, it's me. He wasn't after me; he was after my brother." He did not say another word. It just seemed like one thing after another with Bud.

One day, he had gone to the back side of the pasture to herd cows, and his sight left him; he went completely blind in the middle of a field, wondering and stumbling as he tried to find his way. There was a shaggy dog that followed Bud. Bud took hold of the dog, and when Bud tried to go in the opposite direction from the barn or dairy, the dog would not move. But when he would walk toward the dairy, the dog would walk with him. The dog led him to a fence, and Bud followed the fence to the barn. There, his brother spotted him and knew something was wrong.

They took Bud to the hospital and found that blood clots from a combination of things, the gunshots, and the three spots in his head, trickled the blindness. He would sleep sitting up in a recliner chair. He did this for months. After some time, Bud got better; he went back to believing in himself and realizing that he is supposed to have something out of life.

He wanted and was determined to have a home of his own, plus whatever else he could get his hands on. So, he invested a few dollars he had collected over time from shine sales. He and Charley King, Millie's boyfriend, built them a liquor still on the backside of the dairy's pasture, in a wooded, remote area.

The area was thick with trees and forestry. It was so dense that a cow or dog would have a difficult time trying to get through the brush. So, a person would never find the liquor still unless Bud or Charley showed them the entrance. They had did a great job camouflaging the entry.

Then Bud and Charley went into Jacksonville and rented a boarding house, turned it into a Juke with rental rooms; it had at least six rooms. The club was called Bud's. He had bands to perform with, and it was a jamming place. The women would turn tricks, and the men would rent a room to do their thing with the prostitutes. Bud got his cut from the women, as if he were pimping. However, that was not the case; Bud just wanted a financial stake in the action.

They were taking house money from the gambling games, whether it was dice or cards. Bud moved a lot of his shine, and all that he could not provide; the local police would deliver theirs in two five-gallon gas cans.

They were doing it up, living large for a black man. Bud made it, he felt.Bud moved to Baldwin, Florida, and went to work for Harley Spence. Bud had things going his way. There, he purchased five acres and built a nine-room home just down from the theater, and he had a small pond in the backyard.

He took in a young white man named Stoney Brooks. Bud took him in, like he was his own son. Bud gave him a job; the only thing about Stony was that he didn't stay in one place very long. Stony liked to run after rich White women from the beach area. He would tell Bud how he would dog them out, and make them fools for him, then dump them.

They all would hang out at Bud's juke in Big Jack. They had all the fun they could, letting the good times roll, playing songs like "Darling You Send Me" by Sam Cooke and "I Am The Back Door Man" by Willie Dixon.

The club was really jumping, and Bud was doing very well until Millie and a few others quit looking after things the way they should, when Bud was running the dairy and could not be there. He didn't allow Ella to participate in anything with the juke, nor his daughters; they were never allowed in any clubs, period. He was a very strict man when it came to his wife and daughters.

There was a time when a stranger came to the dairy and applied for a job. Bud hired the man and put him to work. What Bud didn't know was that the man was working with the Feds. He was one who tried to be a still buster, putting whoever in jail for bootlegging shine. He worked around the dairy for months, drank with them all, and partied with them from time to time. He would work very closely with them to gain their confidence, doing work around Bud's house, such as yard work or fixing up a pen for calves that Bud would have in the back of his yard.

One day, while he was at the club, Bud tested him by letting him receive ten gallons of shine that had been delivered by the police. He saw that Bud was related to crooked cops who needed extra money; after all, this was Big Jack, and anything went. From that point, the man wanted to get more deeply involved in whatever Bud had going on.

Then one day, he got around to tasting some of the shine Bud had run off from his own still and found out about it from the Big O or someone like that. Anyway, he found out that Bud had a still; he knew somebody in the area had liquor stills set up in those woods somewhere close to Big Jack. Bud would never tell him what he had set up because what the man didn't know was that Bud didn't trust him, nor any white man, period.

Despite his relationship with Stony, when people meet Bud, they just couldn't figure him out to save their lives. Bud was just a man, one of a kind. He was very curious; he studied people, especially when they tried to get close to him. Perhaps because he was a fugitive, hiding from the law, he believed they were after him. The man began to snoop around, asking everyone specific questions about Bud. They would tell Bud that the man had asked about him, and Bud would ask them what he had said, then Bud would wonder about the guy.

One day, the man asked about the still. He said, 'I know you got one, because I've drunk some of the shine.' It drank real smooth; it was some of the best I ever had. He told Bud he had some people who would pay top dollar, but they needed quite a bit. 'How big of a still you got?" Bud would not respond; he acted like he didn't hear the guy. At that time, his brother James came up and wanted him to take him to town.

Then, shortly after that, Bud met with his partner, Mr. Charlie King, and they suspected that the guy might be a nark trying to bust them. Charlie said he had been snooping for a time now. Have you told him anything? Bud responded, "No, hell no, I ain't said a word. He told me I had a still, and that he done drank some of the liquor from it. Now, who told him? I would like to know?"

They decided to go out to the still. Once they got out there, they built a fire and sat around it, and started sippin' on that shine. And there they began to plan on what they were going to do about the guy. Well, they made a plan on how to get rid of him once they found out he was a nark. They dug a deep hole, about five feet deep, and at least seven feet long. They covered it with brush, palmetto fronds, and grass, so it would not look obvious.

They would never drink to the point of staggering at all, just enough to be tight. While they were in the woods, Bud would practice shooting his .45 and .38 in the moonlight, so he could shoot. They were determined to kill this guy if he proved to be who they suspected him to be. Charlie knew Bud was going to do it, and he knew that if he did, he'd better keep his tongue and forever take this to his grave.

They went back to their activities. Bud worked at the dairy and went to see about his family, as if that was the only thing he was doing. Then the man came to Bud again and told him that his people were ready, and that he done told them that he might be able to get them some of the best shine in the south. He wanted to know if Bud was ready to do business. Bud told him to let him think about it, and he would let him know.

Bud immediately got in touch with his friends from the police department and asked them about anyone in their department or surrounding counties who were narks or Feds looking for stills. They told him that they had heard the feds were up to something in the area, but they didn't know what it was. That's all it took for Bud and his friend to set the guy up to meet with them, so that they could sell him the shine.

They were going to get the money and sell him the shine that the police delivered, and never show him the still. All he needed was liquor, that's all, he doesn't need to know where a bout's shine comes from, as long as it's good. The shine the officers sold Bud was from the white operators in the county, and their liquor was some of the best. So, when Bud set up the deal, the man insisted on seeing the still; he wanted in on the business dealings. He kept on until Bud gave in; he told the man that he would let him know when. So, Bud got in touch with Charlie King, and they decided to carry out their plan: take him out.

They agreed to do it on a Friday night when everyone was busy having a fun time spending money. It's Friday, payday. Around 9:30 p.m. that Friday night, they all went to the still; Bud had the man to know at a moment's notice. They picked the man up, told him to ride with them, and the man got in a truck they had and went to the woods.

They went to a spot and parked, then they had to walk about an eighth of a mile to the spot where they knew they would find the opening that led to the place where they cut out and set up the still. Once they got out there, Bud showed the man the still, and they sat around and drank a while. Charlie said he had to pee, so he stepped off into the dark, woody area. Bud and the man talked for a minute or two. Bud told him that he had something to show him.

Then he walked him over to the place where he and Charlie had dug the grave. Supposedly, Charlie rushed up behind the guy and hit him on the back of the head with a shovel. The man fell on top of the brush into the hole. The man's eyes popped open as Bud threw the first shovel full of dirt in his face. They kept on shoveling dirt until he was covered, and they filled the hole. They buried him alive and packed up their liquor and destroyed the steel, and that ended the still business. They resumed life as if everything was okay, no one knew anything, and they surely would not tell a living soul.

———————◆———————

Time moved on, and Bud kept his club running for a few more years before letting it go due to a lack of business. He ran the dairy and sold calves that he raised to earn extra money; he did very well at this. Not only would he sell his stock, but he would also sell anything that belonged to anybody. He sold Bo's car, bought a new one, and gave it to his wife. Before she could get used to driving it, Bud sold it.

One day, a man came to the dairy. He was looking for cattle to buy and wanted to know who he needed to see to purchase some cows. Bud told the man that he was the man he needed to see. He took the man and showed him a herd of cows, telling the man that he would sell him as many as he wanted.

The man said he wanted about fifty heads. Bud told the man to give him $300.00 per head, and he would start with the sale of ten at the time, which came to $3,000.00. The man paid Bud up front and wanted to know what time to come pick them up, or if he could pick them up then. Bud told the guy to come really late in the evening and pull the trailer up to the pen in the pasture where he would show him. Then, just count off the ten he wanted, load them up, and take them out. The man said, 'We got a deal.' They shook hands and sealed it.

Late that afternoon, the man arrived with his trailer and backed it up to the pen, where he began rounding up the cows he wanted from the herd. While he was sorting out the cattle, picking out the best-looking ones, Mr. Carter saw the trailer pull up to his pen. He went and asked Bud what was going on. Bud asked him what he meant.

Carter said, "I see this trailer down at the pasture backed up to the pen, and it looks like some guy is trying to load some of my cows on it."

Bud said. "What? You better call the law 'cause some son of a## is down there stealing our cows."

Mr. Carter called the law, while he was waiting for the law to come, he went down there and yelled at the man, and asked him, "What the hell are you doing in my darn field rustling. I got the law on its way, I'm putting your butt in jail just as show as they get here."

The man said that black, then he jumped into his truck and fled off like his rear was on fire. By that time, Bud came cruising by just as if everything was ok, raised his hand and waved at Mr. Carter as he passed by with his Dobb hat broke down on one side of his head. Well, the man and Bud were gone by the time the law came, and Mr. Carter kind of figured that Bud had something to do with the man stealing the cows.

When Carter saw Bud the next day he asked him about the situation at the pin, Bud was walking carrying some milk machines in his hand into the barn, he stops looked Mr. Carter in the eyes and said I don't know, I don't know why he was doing that, he should have known better, see I don't have any cows them yours, and hell that man knew better. Trying to take our cows. Bud went on into the dairy and resumed his work with a part of the money in his pocket. Bud didn't see that fellow anymore, and he continued raising his own calves.

Bud took calves from the dairy as if they were his own. He could do this because he was over the dairy. When a cow had a calf, Bud would record the calf's birth as a stillborn or simply not record the birth at all. After a few years had passed, Mary and her husband, Earl Shanks, relocated to Indiantown, Florida, and began working for Norman Hales at Hales Dairy. Meanwhile, Chester got married and decided to move away from the dairy. Chester and his wife, Minnie, moved to Indiantown, Florida. Minnie was a beautiful black woman with a light brown complexion.

Chester loved her very much; he was like Bud; he didn't play. But he would do anything for you, the act of kindness from his heart.He just didn't play. There was a time when he bought a brand-new Chevrolet Impala Sport. He went out to the small town, which was a seasonal area known as Booker Park. Booker Park was lawless, located twenty miles west of Stuart, Florida, twenty-six miles south of Okeechobee, thirty-three miles north of West Palm Beach, Florida, and forty-two miles east of Belle Glades, Florida, also twenty-three miles from Pahokee, Florida.

There was no hospital in Indiantown; the nearest one was in Stuart, Florida. This place, called Indiantown, was surrounded by Groves and sugar cane fields. The biggest operation other than the groves was Hales Dairy. Of course, Chester lived and worked at the dairy; he was what you called the feed man because he mixed the feed for the cows to eat while they were being milked. He also occasionally ran the milk machine. Chester had a nice sixty-five-foot mobile home; he believed in class, like Bud. The Impala was a soft, light canary yellow with a black top and a snow-white interior.

One evening, Chester went to Booker Park to Hamp's juke joint, a real dangerous place with nasty restrooms. It was the gateway to hell for some; men would get killed in this place, after all, it was lawless, under the county, and they were headed out of Stuart, 20 miles away. Bodies would be found in the groves, and the serial killer Schaefer was from Martin County. This was a place.

Well, Chester had too much to drink, and unbeknownst to him, there was another automobile in Booker Park, just like his, the same year, make, and model. The only thing was that it belonged to a Mexican from Palm Beach County.

When Chester got ready to get in his car (so he thought), which was not his but the Mexican's car. There, the man sat under the driver's seat. Chester said, 'Hey, what are you doing in my car?' and told the man to get out, but the man would not move. Chester grabbed the guy and tried to get him out, but the man would not move; he held on to the stern wheel.

Chester said the hell with this, pulled out his pistol, and stuck it in the man's mouth, breaking out one of the guy's front teeth. He held the gun in the man's mouth and was bringing him out when someone who knew him said Hey, Chester, your car is over there. This is that man's car.

Chester became so embarrassed that he didn't know how to do anything other than say, 'I'm sorry.' The poor Spanish guy could only respond by saying mucho loco because he couldn't speak English. Well, Chester decided that the evening had been spoiled by his own actions and that he was better off going home.

Chester had a wonderful relationship with his wife, and they would work together at times. He allowed her to have her freedom, and she would sometimes go to Booker Park.One day, while she was there, she met a young man named Theodor, who was tall and handsome to her. Somehow, she got involved with him and started a romantic relationship. She would let him drive Chester's new car all over town; she was deeply involved with Theodor.

She really got very open, as if she really didn't care about people talking about what she was doing. One Monday evening, Theodor sent a note to Chester's wife through his cousin Jim Cobb, who lived in a trailer about 25 feet behind Chester's trailer. Instead of Mr. Jim giving the note to her, he gave it to Chester's boss.

The next day, while working, Chester's boss took the note and began teasing Chester. Saying Chester, I thought you said that was a one-man's car. Chester told his boss, "That's right, it's a one-man's car." His boss said, "Take a look at this." He showed Chester the letter.

I'll be there to pick you up on Friday, baby.

It devastated Chester; his heart was broken, shattered into a million pieces, and all he could do was drop his head. From that deep pain, a vengeance rose from within his cold, cold trait. It was that killer that dwelled within him, that he didn't know he had; it arose to the surface, and took over him.

It led him; he drove all the way back to North Florida, where Bud and Ella were. He tried to get them to keep his two children. He didn't tell them what was going on with him. Bud told Ella that something was wrong, that boy don't look right, better not keep them children. Well, he left them and went to Valdosta and tried to get his sister and Man Shanks to keep them, and they refused as well; it seemed like everyone picked up on Chester just was not the same as they knew him.

While he was in Georgia, he purchased a 12-gauge automatic shotgun with a full choke on the end of the barrel and several boxes of double-aught 3-inch buckshot; he was gearing up for what he was planning to do.

He was hurt beyond expression. When he tried to sleep, he would see them in his mind making love. The days passed, and he went back home, managing to act as if he didn't have the note. That Friday finally came. Chester got up and didn't go to work, as he had the whole week off.

Minnie asked him, 'Honey, you aren't going to work today.'

'I think I'm going to stay home and spend this time with you.' Then Chester went and came out with the shotgun from the back room.

'You got a new gun?'

He said, 'Yes, I got it for you and your man.'

She laughed and said, "My man? What are you talking about?"

He took the butt of the gun and knocked out all her front teeth and said, "The one that sent this note to your butt. And I'm going to kill the son of a -when he comes."

"You've taken me for a darn fool! If he doesn't come, I'm going to kill your butt anyway."

Well, Theodor showed up. Chester said, 'Is that him? Is that him!' Minnie said, "Chester, please don't kill him, please!"

When Theodor went to walk over to his cousin's house, where he had given the note, he was totally unaware of what his cousin had done. When he got about halfway to the trailer, Chester saw him from the side window of his trailer. Open the window and call unto him, "Hey, you."

When Theodor turned to see who called him, Chester shot him in the face with that 12-gauge loaded with double-aught buckshot. The shot cut the brim of his cap, and took out his right eye and a third of his face. Theodor broke and ran. Chester shot him in the back, blew a hole that you could see through. Theodor fell to one knee and begged for his life, "Man, please don't kill me." Chester stuck the gun to Theodor's upper body and unloaded another round into Theodor's chest.

Then he grabbed Minnie by the head from her hair, and said, "Look at that pretty face now," and then he shot him twice more in the face. Chester blew Theodor's face from between his ears. The only thing left was skin and a portion of his scalp. Of course, you know Minnie ran with all her might. She jumped an 8-foot fence, running for her life. She went to the dairy farm and hid in Mr. Hale's Office under the desk. Chester took his time and walked to the dairy, and as he looked for his wife, his 5-year-old daughter followed him.

When he found Minnie, she gave herself away; her head was bumping the desk, caused by her shaking with fear. Chester aimed the gun at her head, and his daughter grabbed him by the pant leg and said, "Daddy, please don't kill my mama." That took his nerve, he told her, 'You better love this child all the days you have, because I supposed to kill you.'

He went back to his trailer and leaned his gun by the door, and yelled with a loud voice as he sobbed in tears from the act of an unforgiven love.

His brother Bo was a witness to this brutal killing; it will always be in his mind, what is in him, the trait of the DNA, a bloodline of good people. It's sad how life and love can get so entangled, the thin line between love and hate.

Mary, Chester's sister, was screaming, "My brother just killed a man, Oh God, what has he done." This was a very dark day at the dairy, which gave them the name 'the dairy people'. The law came and picked up Chester. He went to jail, and there was no bond set for him to bail out; he got a twenty-year sentence. That was a terrible setback for the family; everybody in the family hated what Chester had done, but we all still loved him, and that did not change.

It was just a misfortune that had happened. Things can go so wrong, but one has to move on, and that's how it went. This was the typical trait of brutality that stirs deep down in the Black man's soul and spirit. The instinct to kill, be blind sighted by hate mingled with love and rage, to the point that a human life has no value, just snuff it out, the way he did. Then the courts were no better- twenty years for that heinous type of crime.

If he had killed a white man in the manner he did, he would have gotten the electric chair or life in prison. Chester got out in four years. Life is so strange. Down through the years, Terrie, his sister, became best friends with the victim's sister-in-law, whose name was Mary. Terrie's friend Mary, a few years later, died, and her children communicated with Terrie for the rest of her life.

It seems like the murky lifestyle for the Black man is an affixed scenario. The lack of emotional control, trying to hold in the demon that lurks deep within, behind the conscience, of the mind of man. It seems like the lyrics in a Tupac song: 'I am not the killer, but don't push me.'

Trapped in the Bubble.

Chester got out of prison and went to where Bud and his father were, and they had a long conversation about what he had encountered while he was in prison. Chester told them about how the correctional officer ate a breakfast he had cooked, and fell dead. Then he talked about how he wanted to get a new start on life.

Bud told him to go back to work at the dairy or somewhere else, and just do the best he could, to start over. Believe it or not, he got back together with the same woman, but it didn't work out. Minnie still had those bad traits of doing the wrong thing. Something went on with big Benny Webbs.

Chester found out about it and came to me. He and I were the best of friends; he asked me to help him kill Big Benny because Benny had disrespected him. So, he went out and got a 55-gallon drum to put his body in, but Big Benny got the word that Chester was looking for him, so he hid from him.

That gave me a chance to talk with Chester; I told him, 'Man, look what you're doing. This same woman you went to prison for is doing the same thing, so let it go.' He acted as if he would let it go, and we stopped looking for Big Benny and went home.

Then, late one evening, Chester spotted Benny at a club, pulled out his pistol, pointed it in Benny's face, and told him to get down on the ground, on all fours, now bark like a dog, that you are. Big Benny knew who Chester was and what he was capable of doing, so he got down and started barking like a dog. Chester stuck his gun in his face and said, "Look, don't you ever cross me again."

Then he went home and packed all his rags and left that woman for good. After he left her and time passed, he met a young girl who was a pretty good person. The only problem was that sometime after she got with Chester and he went on with his life, he and I stopped being the best of friends because of the type of people he wanted to socialize with, and I just did not like those people, so our relationship somewhat changed. I still thought as much of him as I always had, but I just couldn't roll with his new crew, so distance came between us.

He started dealing drugs, selling crack, and became one of the biggest dealers in Okeechobee, FL. The young lady he took as a companion got on crack, and man, did he have a problem on his hands. She got really bad and became a heavy smoker. She would do things like sell the drawers *off her children* that Chester just paid for, or sell the new items just purchased for their children. They had been together for years, and now they had four children. She got so bad that she sold the furniture out of the house to a Haitian.

Chester came home, and the house was empty. He took her to find the person she had sold it to, but he refused to give up the furniture. Chester asked him to return his furniture. The guy said No way, Chester acted as if he was about to walk away, turned about, took his pistol, and stuck it to the man's head, and asked him, "Do you want to die or live?" The man said, 'Live,' and Chester told him he had one hour to get the furniture back to his house. The furniture was returned, but the issues did not end there with her; she just had a problem.

One night, when Chester went to work, she took a young man to the house, and Chester caught them there. He made the young man leave, then he took a knife from the kitchen, set her down, took the knife, and dragged it across her face. He had a whetstone rock sharpen the blade and commenced to drag it again; he did this until her whole face was lacerated. Then he made her take a handful of salt and wash her face. The last time he wrapped her in barbed wire, he beat her with a two-by-four and left her outside all night. His neighbor found her and unwrapped her.

After all she went through, she didn't change, so Chester gave up on trying to do anything. He realized that what he was doing was wrong and that the drug had total possession and control of her. And there was nothing anyone could do to help her. She loved her children, and they loved her, but that didn't make a difference. He just let her go, and she remained in that condition until she died.

See, so many people fall through the seams of life due to drugs, especially good people. She was a real unique person in her own way; she was just a victim of drugs. She came from a particularly good family. All of their children turned out to be very good people. Her daughter is a beautiful, spirited, and hardworking young lady; she's a manager at a McDonald's.

Trapped in the bubble, that old life cycle,
the circle of time, trying to survive the turbulence of it all.

Chester's life was transformed by love. It's funny how people's lives can get so far off track. It makes you wonder why the harder you try, the worse it gets. You have to look at the positive side of things and overrule the negative portion with joy and love. You must focus on something positive by reaching deep within and finding some means of hope, love, and tranquility.

The Bubble of time and hardships, Chester died from AIDS. Inside that Bubble, his death was slow and pain-filled. He got down to around 85 pounds; the skin on his lips peeled off as if it were flakes. But the woman he loved so much, who made him kill a man, she lived to be an old woman. I imagine she had a horrific romantic story she could have told, but she kept it concealed until the day she died.

CHAPTER

6

Now, let me get back to Bud. Well, as a few years passed and life returned to normal, Bud settled down a lot, but he still loved women, just like Uncle James, his brother.

There was this lady called Jean who was the Big O's girlfriend, but when she got to drinking, she would fool around with Bud and Uncle James. And knowing them, they all would drink, then they would fool around; Jean would pull her dress up and flash the fellows with her pretty legs.

Boy, they would react like a hound, like when a dog is in heat. The Big O would act up some, but he really didn't care; she was just short of being the circles. However, there was another man named Mr. Johnny Curry, who was in love with Miss Jean; it was good to him, and he thought Bud was going out with Jean.

Meanwhile, Big O met Katherine Jones, and she was a girl who didn't really care one way or the other. She was a very unique person; she just loved herself some men. There was a time when she had an affair with a young man named Jean Scrappy, during the same time she was living with Big O.

So late, one evening, he sent her to the store to get him a six-pack of Colt 45 beer. He loved that beer; it was the only beer he would drink. Something happened that made her stay gone too long for him. When she got back, he asked her if she had his beer, the very moment that she answered him.

He took his time and pulled out his Barlow knife, opening it as he pulled it from his pocket. Then wacked her under the chin went the knife. Blood spurted out everywhere. She ran inside, got a towel, and pressed it directly to the wound. Well, Bud and Ella took her to the hospital, where she received about nine stitches.

The Big O, they called him, had found out about the affair, but really didn't want anyone to know that he knew about the affair, and that was his reason for cutting her. She went along with him, after cutting her, for like a couple of months. We all thought she had forgiven him, but weren't we wrong.

She took her time and put a 10-quart foot tub filled with water. She put it on the stove, then let it boil down about an inch and a half in the foot tub. She went into the living room, where Big O was lying down, reading a Playboy magazine with his feet propped up toward the door.

He had the book in front of his face and could not see her or what she was holding. She said, 'You whoo, you whoo, darling sweetheart, I got something for you.' When he looked up to see what she had, the moment he saw it, she dashed the entire tub of boiling hot water on him. He jumped up and took off after her. He took the knife and raised it above his head as he chased after her.

When they had run about 150 yards, she turned to the left; he turned to the right, running as hard as he could, trying to get the wind to cool him down from the heat of the burn. Bud and them took the car and caught up with him, trying to get him to get in so they could take him to the doctor. But he kept rolling and yelled out, 'You're going too slow.'

When they finally got him to get in the car, as they approached the red light, he'd yell, 'Run it, run it, please! The wind is blowing.'

That was a sad sight to see; blisters the size of four-inch balloons popping out all over his body. It took a long time for him to heal, and that ultimately ended the relationship between them.

One day, Bud, Uncle James, Joe Hamilton, and Johnny Curry's brother went to a little club with one way in and one way out. Everybody was having such a good time, dancing and enjoying each other's company, the way black folks socialized, other than the way they have church.

They knew how to party, they let it all hang out, with clean shaves, some with processed hair, and some with plain, o'nappy heads. They all wanted to look sporty and show a whole lot of soul; the brothers got down, and so did the sisters. They were dressed really sexy and would throw down on the floor, dancing in a nasty and classical way.

They were having a real good time. Bud was leaning on the counter with one foot on the foot prop, talking to the bartender, just shooting the breeze. He was wearing his Dobbs hat broke down on one side. He wore it tilted on one side like a real gangster, wearing a blue surd suit with floor shine shoes, he had a gold tooth in his mouth, a diamond ring on his finger, and a gold chain in his belt loop. Bud was clean.

Mr. Johnny Curry walked through the door of the club and shot Bud in the back on his lower left side. The bullet lifted Bud, then laid him on the counter facing the bartender. Bud pushed himself from the counter as he began to turn.

Mr. Curry hit him again with that ring nose 38; it cut a groove across Bud's back, causing him to buckle backwards. Bud continued to turn to see who was capping him like that. When he turned about, Curry hit him again just above the heart on his left side, which laid Bud back over the counter.

The bartender had hit the floor, hiding from the flying bullets in the place. Bud struggled for his pistol, a six-inch-barreled .38, as he was coming down from the counter. As he came down, Mr. Curry hit him again on the right side of his chest and laid him back on the counter.

Curry got off one more shot, which creased Bud on the side. That time, Bud shot at Curry and missed him, but the next shot, Bud hit him directly in his belly button. Curry's mouth flew open very wide, and he dropped the gun, Curry's brother said you shot my brother, then Bud turned and shot him in the arm. He broke camp and ran from the club.

Bud walked up to Johnny Curry and shot him in the chest above his heart, then again in the chest on the right side, then shot him everywhere he had shot him. He threw up his hand above his head to come down for the kill shot, and the roller jumped out of the gun.

Bud saw his son-in-law with both arms and legs against the door bar that was bracing the back door. Then, by some unknown strength, Bud was able to walk out, get to his car, and drive home. When he got home, his daughter, Terrie, rushed up to the car to see if he had brought her something from the store.

Terrie got to the car and saw all the blood. She ran back inside, where her mother was yelling Daddy is dead. Ella rushed outside, where Bud was, and saw that he was in a mess; she had him move over. She drove him to the hospital in Jacksonville, Florida. There, he was placed in intensive care. Believe it or not, they brought Mr. Curry in and put him in the same room with Bud. That was a big mistake.

When Bud came around and realized who was in the room with him, he immediately got up with all the lines attached to him and went for Curry. Curry went into screaming and yelling for his life, Get me out! Get me out of here. Then the doctor and the nurses realized these two men had done this to the other. So they separated them, placing Curry into another room.

As soon as they were well enough to come to court, they had to appear. The Judge asked each one of them if they were going to get another gun, given what they had just gone through. All the pain was caused by guns.

When the judge turned and asked Bud directly, 'Are you going to get another gun, Mr. Wright?' Bud's response was, 'Just as soon as I leave here today.'

After that, Bud calmed down a lot. He was older. While he was out of commission, he quit the dairy and moved to Indiantown, Florida. His daughter, Freddy, and her husband, Elder Shanks, had moved from Georgia to Hales Dairy. Bud and Ella moved in with them while Bud was recovering from the gunshot wounds.

As the months passed, during this time, he was able to go fishing; they would use regular worms and catch a lot of bass, bluegill, and brim. Nice-sized bass, ranging from 1 pound to 8 pounds, were caught. There were times when they would go fishing for speckle perch or crappie in Lake Okeechobee.

The fishing is excellent in South Florida, especially the saltwater fishing. Bud would go hunting in the orange groves, where the rabbits are plentiful. He started practicing with his pistol to go back and get Johnny Curry for shooting him; he said he was shot for no reason. He got to the point that he'll see a rabbit 50 yards away, he'll draw aim for a split second, and fire, and 7 of 10 rabbits would have head shots. He was getting better and better each time we went out to the groves.

After he recovered, he went to Norman Hales for a job at the dairy, and Norman Hales hired him. He gave him the job as a booger boy, a person who rounds up the cows to be milked. At the dairies, you have five cattle pens on each side of the dairy, five on the east side, and five on the west side.

This typically consists of five different herds of cows, mostly Holsteins, in four of the pens or pastures, and one herd of Jerseys for butter fat in the fifth pasture. The dairy never shuts down, regardless of the weather conditions or any other reason, except for a power failure or a common breakdown. The cows had to be milked and always maintained, and it was long hours of hard work running the milk machine in flat barns.

At this point, Bud is now older, shot up, and trying to get over the best way he can. The world has changed; the Civil Rights Movement is a heavy reality, and Dr. Martin Luther King is doing his thing, letting freedom ring from every rooftop, every valley, from every clay hill of Georgia, throughout America.

Artists like James Brown, say it aloud, I'm black and I'm proud, songs like that filled the airwaves. Groups like The Imperials sang songs like, *'If you had a choice of color, which one would you choose, my brother?'*

Yes, America was going through some real changes, for race relations, the Black man's quest for Justice and Equality under the law, working on the lowest scale, living below poverty. Dealing with the new world was not easy.

The air was filled with hatred; you could feel the intensity. There was a reluctant odor of unkindness everywhere. People still lived separately; black people could not afford to live in upper-class houses or apartments. Very few could at that time; things were rough for the majority. Bud, with no education, found it extremely hard to maneuver about and fit in, but he had what they called "mother wit." He knew how to survive in this harsh world environment.

Years passed, and Bud and Momma grew older. Bud's brother, David Wright, had a son, and one day, his son fell ill. They went to see him on his dying bed. He was just lying there. Bud and Bud's daughter, Janey, went to visit him. His name was Dave. He began to tell me things about his life, some things, I guess he just had to say before he died.

He turned to Bud and asked him, Bud, just how many people did you kill? He said, "Bud, do you remember you killed the man because he caught you with his wife, and you throwed the man into the pond behind the church. And they could not find the body because it was bottomless, do you remember that, Bud?"

Bud reached, got a pillow, and put it over the man's face and pressed down on it really hard. Janey came into the room and spotted Bud with the pillow over her cousin's head, covering his face.

She rushes up to Bud and says, "Daddy, daddy, stop, you are killing the man."

Bud said, "Hell, that's what I'm trying to do if you let me. He was just lying, I reckon."

Well, she got Bud to stop, and Bud leaned over and whispered something into the man's ear. Then he said out loud, "Take it to the grave when you go." That was the kind of fellow Bud was.

Time passed, and we all went out together. One day, we went out to a club called Mr. JD's. We sat down in the club. This was the first time Bud had a car that wasn't a Cadillac; he owned a Ford.

Well, his son-in-laws were with him, having a drink, and Robert, one of them, owed Bud a dollar. Bud asked him for it, and Robert told him he was taking the dollar; in other words, he wasn't giving it back. That's all it took.

I went to the car, reached under the seat, got Bud's pistol, and took out all the bullets. Because I knew how Bud was, he was a fun person to be around. But he would snap at a moment's notice, especially when he felt being taken advantage of, regardless of who you were. I don't know if it came from the three holes that were drilled in his head from the wreck years back, or if Bud was just mean.

Bud jumped up and rushed to his car to leave, but Robert jumped in the car as well. I got in the seat next to Bud. Bud felt under the seat and grabbed his seven-shot .22 Magnum. Then reached across me, stuck the gun to the center of Roberts' chest, and pulled the trigger several times. He threw the gun to the floor of the car, then jumped from the car and walked home. I took the car home. Robert stretched his eyes really wide from fear, and cocked his foot, like a gun, toward the north star, pulled up, and took off running as hard and as fast as he could.

Please don't get the wrong picture of Bud; he was a very good man, but he could be dangerous when upset. I loved the ground he walked on; he would at times make you laugh until water flowed from both eyes. He told me a story about when he and brothers were little boys growing up; his mother was something else.

They were playing "dog catch the coon." His brother Leroy was the raccoon, James was the hound, Cal was the master, and Bud was just a team player with Calvin. Well, James treed the raccoon, which was Leroy. James walked really slow anyway,–closed his eyes, tilted his head back, facing upward, Leroy dropped his pants, and unloaded a soupy mess directly into James' face, splash. James screamed as loud as he could, Momma. She ran outside to see what had happened.

That's when James says, 'Look, Momma, Leroy dookied in my face.' She cleans him up, then she beats Leroy, I mean, a real whipping. She tells Leroy every time he tells me that he smells dookie, I'm going to beat your ass like you stole something. Well, one morning, after a year had past, James said, 'Mamma, I can smell it.' She gets up and whips Leroy like the first time.

Can you believe that a year later,
she would react as if it had just happened?

JOHN ROBINSON

*N*ow let me tell you about how I met Mr. Bud Wright, someone
that I love to this present day.

When I met Mr. Bud, I had just turned 14. I was fresh out of
trouble, coming from Benton Harbor, Michigan, where I attended
the Pioneer School for boys. A school run and operated by a man
named David Mullins, my hero to this day. He changed my life,
took me off the road of destruction, and placed me on another
path. One that would pack my mind with wisdom, through this
passage of being trapped in the bubble.

If it hadn't been for the fact that he set me free from that Bubble of entrapment. I was given five years. Mr. Mullins intervened,
took me from jail, and allowed me to be a part of his experimental
boys' school program. Anyway, he set me free, and we went to Baton Rouge, Louisiana, then to South Florida, where I met Mr. Bud.

Baton Rouge was a territorial city; whatever side you lived on
as a young person, you did not dare go to the other side. If you
did, you might not get back home, or you had to fight in the hood
to survive. This was a city of gumbo and red beans and rice, but
once you get used to the city, you learn to cope with the conditions or living arrangements.

I had been a troubled child from abuse, and Mr. Bud filled the void, the lack of love, that was missing from my life. We would go fishing all the time to enjoy the days as they passed, and we had some terrific times. Bud was older and calmer, probably due to aging, but still, he was Bud. He would explain to me how life was and what to expect as I merged into manhood. He would always tell me that a man was a man and to treat all men and women with respect, expecting the same in return. As I lived with them, believe me, I grew to know Bud Wright and loved him as a Father.

I recall a time when we lived on the line at Norman Hales' dairy, where Bud was the booger boy rounding up the cows to be milked inside the dairy. Well, Bo Bud's youngest son, known as Bo Wright, operated the milk machines. Chester had gotten out of prison for killing the man Theodor. It was amazing how Chester managed to get out of prison.

There was a security guard in the prison who, every morning, would come into the mess hall where all the prisoners would be eating their breakfast, and Chester was the cook. Well, this particular morning, the guard came in and didn't say what he always says when he comes into the mess hall," give me some steak and eggs," that he didn't say; he just sat down and took a bite of sausage and fell dead.

An inmate who was a paramedic revived the guard, who died later from a heart attack. The inmate was set free the same day. He told the warden that Chester helped him revive the guard, and they gave Chester his walking papers three weeks later. Chester said he thought somebody had done something to his food that he had cooked that morning in the prison. He found out that the guard had a heart attack; that's the story of how Chester got out of prison for such a heinous crime.

Anyway, Chester was working in the dairy, along with several other men, running milk machines. Norman Hales was hard to deal with; he had a real nasty attitude toward people in general. One day, I went to him for a job, and he told me to get to work right now if I wanted the job. I told him that I would start the following day. He bent over and got about a half inch from my ear and yelled as loud as he could, "Get to running them machines, I mean right now."

Well, I stepped away from him and told him, "Don't yell in my ear like that." He said, 'Get the hell off my Dairy right now.' As I was walking off and came past the feed room, I saw Chester, and I stopped to talk with him for a few minutes. By that time, Big Norman Hales walked out and looked toward the east, then toward the north, and then to the south, and spotted me. He acted as if he was trying to find out which way for me to go once he started.

'I thought I told you to get, didn't you hear me?'

I turned and told Chester, 'Wait one minute, let me let this man know something.'

I charged toward this giant, got to him, and looked up, dead into his face, and asked, 'What are you going to do?' He was shocked.

I said, 'That's what I thought. You'll be better off calling the police, and when they come, tell them not to disturb me if I'm eating my breakfast. I'll be at my uncle Earl's house when they come.'

I walked away from him as I headed toward my uncle's house. His wife, Aunt Mary, said, 'Don't step a foot on the porch; let it land on the back of the truck.' That was to get me away from there as quickly as she could.

Norman Hales was a nasty man to work for, but you had to let him know that you were not scared of him. He would sneak around the dairy, trying to find a reason to mess with his employees. One night, big Norman Hales sneaked into the feed room where he could spy on the men working, to see who was drinking alcohol on his job. He looked and saw a man beating one of his cows with a water hose with the nozzle on the end of the hose.

Norman couldn't take it. He broke and ran into the dairy, grabbed the man, who weighed around 150 pounds, and he was soaking wet. Norman took the hoses from the guy and started beating him with the hose the same way he was beating the cow, I mean, he was beating him, then he threw him to the ground, and yelled milk them dam cows.

The guy started running the machines like he had never ran them before. Hales then went up and down the dairy, harassing the rest of the men. When he got to Chester, he said, 'I'm not talking to you, Chester; it's the rest of them I'm after.' He knew what Chester had done; he was not that brave.

He went into the bathroom and caught Big Benny Webb on the toilet stool asleep. He took and kicked him in the rear, cursed at him, and told him to get back in the barn and milk them cows. Big Benny jumped up off the toilet and didn't even clean up, just pulled up his pants and went back to work milking them cows.

Then big Norman Hales went on down to the barn, took his finger, and pointed it at Bo's face, saying, 'It goes for you too.' The only problem was that he had touched Bo in the face. 'What did he go do that for?' All hell broke loose right then. Norman had to run for his life, I mean, run like he never had before, because Bo was on him.

Bo took one of the milk machines and snatched the lines off it, took the round part that was about the size of a baseball, and threw it at Norman Hales as hard as he could throw it. Big Norman ducked and kept running, but Bo was just behind him, trying to catch up, but to no avail. Big Norman was running hard and fast; he was, as they say, rolling.

He ran past his car, jumped into a work truck, and went across the field toward where he lived. In the meantime, Bo went home, where we were, and we had to tie him down with ropes. He was out of his everlasting mind; he was just that far gone. The young man was like a madman. The incident occurred around 8 pm that night. But we had to leave Bo tied up with the ropes the rest of the night. I said to myself, what kind of people are these, who get this angry, that you must tie them down for the night.

Well, Bud had missed all the action because he was rounding up the cattle to be milked. When he got back to the barn, he asked where Bo was. Chester told him that the last time he saw Bo, Norman was stretched and stressed out, running for his life.

They all finished working that night, but early the next morning, everybody except Chester met at Bud's house. Earl Shanks, big Benny Webb, and Flap came down to the house to discuss what had happened during the night. They were explaining to Bud what had taken place because he had missed all the action while gathering one of the herds and changing gates to the holding pens or pastures. Before everyone had gathered, Bud had been oiling his 12-gauge shotgun, which was an automatic. Then he leaned it against the door inside, close to where he was sitting; no one could see it because it was behind the wall.

Well, Norman Hales, believe it or not, pulls up in his new, bent-up Oldsmobile and says, "What's going on, Benny? Go home. Big Benny says, 'Yes, sir, Mr. Hales,' and went home. He said, 'Flap, that's all it took.' Flap went home. Then he said, Earl, get in the car, Earl said I'm not going nowhere with you, no, I'm not going.

At that time, Mama Ella spoke up and said, " Earl, get in the car and go home, you got too many children to be put out, and me and Bud don't have no place for you all. Get the hell off his place as soon and quick as you can.' At that point, Hales say's Bud! That's all it took, Mama yelled Run, Mr. Hales, run.

Bud reached behind himself for his shotgun and got it. He took a shot at the car, but Hales was blazing the trail. After that, I witnessed this man sitting by the door wiping his gun down, as he looked up the road for Hales to come back by.

I asked Mom what he was doing, and she said he's going to kill that man when he comes by. I asked her if he could do that. She said yes, he could, and he will. You'll see. She told Terrie and me not to go near Bud, because he was not the same person we knew; he had become a totally different person.

Bud just sat there and gazed down the road in the direction Norman Hales had to travel; it was the only way into town, unless you took a chance going through the orange grove, a place where a dead body showed up almost every week.

Well, down the road came Norman Hales. When he got into view, Bud jumped up with the shotgun, aimed at the car, as he began to pull the trigger. I grabbed the barrel of the gun and pushed it away from the car as it fired, missing the car, sparing Norman's life.

As a result, Bud took the gun and thrust it under my neck, pushed me against the wall, slid me up the wall, until I reached his eye level, and he stood about six foot one or two. He looked me directly in the eye and said, 'Don't you never, ever do that again. Mama Ella was the only one who could get through to him. She was just walking around, talking calmly to Bud, sayin,

> "Buddy boy, don't you hurt that kid, he's just a child, Come on, Buddy boy, that's Louise's son. Come on, Buddy boy, only you can do it. Buddy boy, let it go."

I had never been so shocked in fear for my life as I was at that moment; his eyes were real cold. He snatched the gun from under my neck, and I hit the floor. He hurried to his room and slammed the door shut. He stayed in there for about seven hours. During that time, we didn't even hear a sound from him for quite some time. Then, suddenly, he came out of the room as if nothing had taken place; he was back to being a normal person.

He said, 'Let's go, boy,' and we went for a ride. Bud was a particularly good person for my life; he showed what it was to be a man. Not in a negative manner, just because he is Bud.

How could a man be a man and not be recognized as a man? Bud came from a time when that was the case. A time of hard knocks in a nation without rights, just to be preyed upon. Men like Norman Hales were the promoters, taking advantage of people with lesser power, those who the law had forgotten.

Therefore, a man like Bud was not of the normal or expected behavior of the typical Black male. He would bust a cap, as he would say, 'Boy, I'll bust a cap.' The only thing about Bud is that he meant it. No, he could not stay there with Hales; if so, somebody was hell-bound.

Well, after the family went through the trauma with Norman Hales, we moved from the line to Booker Park, a small Black seasonal Village; owned mainly by its founders, men like Mr. Sandy Montgomery, Mr. Sam Rhodes, and fruit contractors, such as Mr. Buster. They sold land to Mr. Sammy Bright, who later built a variety of seasonal houses or quarters, which included a nightclub and bar.

Clifford owned the Cadillac Club and the majority of the houses along 5th Street in that area or section of Booker Park.

Junior Mack Night owned the other Black store, other than Mr Sandy's store. Mack Rogers, a white man, owned the biggest store in Booker Park and Rogers Quarters, which consisted of camp-style shotgun houses that he rented on a weekly basis. Freddy Pompper owned the other juke and rental houses on the other end of Booker Park. Preacher Thomas also owned a club and restaurant, as well as several houses, and operated the ice cream parlor.

This place was almost lawless; it was the unincorporated areas under the county. A place where, in 1963, a dead body would lie in the street for hours with cars driving around like it was some dead animal waiting to be moved by the county.

The nearest main sheriff's department jail was in Stuart, Florida, some 20 miles away. Indiantown had only a substation, without a holding cell or jail. The law was crooked and corrupted in the worst way. Booker Park changed the family occupation from Dairy Farming to picking fruit, similar to that of migrant workers.

This means a step away from the security of having a secure future in terms of work. Neither Bud nor his family had ever picked fruit, including oranges, grapefruit, lemons, peppers, or watermelons. This was a totally different world for them. You must physically touch every piece of fruit to be paid by the piece for every bushel or box you fill. Blood, sweat, and sometimes hot tears.

Bud got in touch with Mr. Rufus McCone, who was one of the harvesting contractors in the area. We started the new transition of earning a living; it was a struggle for them, but not for me, because I was a migrant worker, having been so for the past five years. I was used to the heat and the cold, plus the harshness associated with it. In this field, education can be minimal; all you need is a Social Security number and to be in good health to pick fruit.

I picked oranges for Frank Farnnel from time to time. During that period, they were paying 37 cents for a box of oranges, which is equivalent to one bushel. You must pick 100 boxes to earn $27.01, which is not easy to do. My average was 73 boxes a day. I eventually reached the point where I could pick 130 boxes, but my average was still 73 boxes, earning $27.01 per 9-hour day, or $162.06 per week.

However, as a family, we would make three times as much. The only way we could survive was to team through a family bond of unity, and work as a team for the benefit of the whole, for the welfare of the family. That meant that everyone was a contributor to the cause and a supporter of one another. We lived from the same pool of money, and we made sure that everyone's needs were met to the best of our ability. Rainy days, being hurt, or any form of strike would affect the pay scale for the week. It was already hard enough.

Then, one year during the harvesting season, Bud got sick with a form of ulcer. He was unable to work at all; he stayed in the hospital for two months. During that time, I worked hard, picking oranges every day, including Sundays, to pay all the bills for his house. My take-home pay was $162.06 per week. I gave it all to Mama to pay the bills. I would buy a pack of cigarettes and a six-pack of beer; that was all I wanted.

Of course, gas was 25 cents a gallon, cigarettes were 35 cents a pack, and beer was under $3.00 a six-pack. Yes, there has been a significant transition in everything from then until now. I was 16 years old when I did this for Bud; it was the least I could do in return for what he had done for me. When Bud got home, he asked Mama how far behind he was with all his bills and with the rent.

She said, "That boy in there worked and paid all your bills and kept everything paid up."

Later, he called me in to see him, and he thanked me for what I had done for him.

I said to him, 'You never charged me one cent for living here with you and your family; you took me like one of your own sons. It was my duty and responsibility.' He just looked at me for a moment and said, 'I do, thank you.'

About five months later, he was back on his feet; his health was better. We went back to working in the groves and having a good time, enjoying each other's company. You take the people who love the taste of orange juice, they never think, nor do they realize, the hardships of the lifestyle for the rich compared to the poor. And the things they do to amuse themselves to cope in what they felt like is an unchangeable world, so they try to make it as less boring.

It appeared as though this time of life was all one could look forward to; people were working, scraping, and trying to get their children educated, so that they would not have to go through what they were going through. They were just Trapped in the Bubble. Earnings was less than half for a Black person than it was for a white person. And some of the whites were catching hell trying to survive, but he or she had it better.

Blacks' days were like the moonless nights, full of darkness. Somehow, through it all, joy was forever present; we took the hardness from the time. We found a way to cope with the method of madness; some would ignore the white style of a lifestyle; and just be a Brother, push forward regardless of the obstacles in life's path, fighting to survive, hoping one day they'd stumble upon justice and equality.

———◆———

One day in the Fall, we started picking lemons for Minute Maid, owned by the Coca-Cola Division. This particular grove was infested with rattlesnakes, the big diamondbacks. The grove needed mowing very badly; the weeds were high, and you couldn't see what was under your feet - your very next step could be on one of these big boys. This was early in the week, so I decided to play a trick on Bud.

I went and picked some dried-out bean plants. These beans sounded like a rattler when you put several into a brown paper bag and shook them around. I took and put my little gimmick together and crawled under a lemon tree. I hid in the tall weeds around the tree. Bud could not see me at all, and as he started picking, I shook the bag really rapidly. Bud heard the sound, and he stopped picking for a moment. I didn't shake the bag until he started back picking. This time, he stopped picking again. When he started back picking, I took a lemon thorn and stuck it on his leg.

He yells out very loud; all shucks, he got me. He turns about in such a manner that the fruit bag he was wearing stood out from the centrifugal force of his turning about so fast. He throws the bag from his shoulder, runs to the car, and gets out the butcher's knife to cut his leg to release the poison. He pulls up his pant leg, takes the knife and starts to cut his leg, and I yell Hold it, and shook the bag, and show the thorn I stuck him with.

Mama yelled, 'Run, boy, run!' Bud turned for his shotgun. I hit the groves, jumping the little five-foot-wide canals for irrigation. I had to run for my life. I ran for about two miles until I reached a wide canal, about 60 feet across. I swam across it, and Bud turned around. That ended my picking for the day.

Man, I was tired from running. I walked home, which was about ten miles from the groves. When Bud got home, he asked Aunt Millie, "Where is that boy?" She said he was in there. When Bud saw me, he said I put your ass to the woods, didn't I, I said Yes, sir, and I'm sorry I did that. My friend, those were the days that I will never forget.

I remember one afternoon when we were riding back from hunting rabbits; Bud was driving, and I was on the passenger side.

All at once, he said, 'Look what the good Lord has sent us.' It was one of Hales' cows with its head stuck through the fence, grazing. Bud hit his brakes and said, 'Move back, boy!' He took the 22 rifle and shot the cow, and said Let's load it into the car.

The only problem was that it was a big cow. It couldn't fit into the car's back seat on the floor with its feet pointed upward, so we struggled being in a hurry, to prevent from being seen. We slipped on the ground trying to deal with the weight of the cow, and our feet kept slipping on the grass. We were struggling with that cow, but we finally managed to load it into the car.

Instead of going straight home, Bud decided to go to the store and get himself some cigarettes. Believe it or not the cow seemed to come back alive. When Bud shot it, he missed the brain, which means he only stunned the cow. The cow went to a yelling and kicking. Bud said, 'Listen, at that son of a, calling my name.' Then he got out of the car and cut the cow's throat, and blood was everywhere. Then we went home and got some help to unload the cow and hang it so we could skin it.

Once we got started, the tree we hung it in was right along the side of the street. You won't believe the police pulled up while we were skinning it and parked. He said, 'Bud, look, that's a nice stock of beef you got there.' Bud said, 'Sho is, I had a hard time getting him here.' I was scared to death when I heard this man talking to the police like that. The police radio alarm went off, saying that something was happening somewhere, and the officer said, 'Y'all enjoy the steaks; I've got to go.' My heart was relieved; I just looked at Papa and said, 'Man, you are something else.'

CHAPTER

8

Well, time moved on a few years later. I recalled going to a Barbecue that was sponsored by Coca-Cola because they owned Minute Maid, the juice plant, and the groves. All the harvesters who work for Coca-Cola were at this event, enjoying themselves while drinking draft beer from the 55-gallon wooden cag. It was ice-cold draft beer.

The president of the company was there mingling in the crowd, walking around with a plate of baked beans, ribs, and potato salad. Bud had taken over the cag of beer and would not let anyone get any beer except for him and me. He said this cag is for me and you, boy, come on, have a drink.

Bud was about half drunk, so Mr. Norris, the president of the Coca-Cola Foods Division, decided to investigate. He walks over to Bud. Before Mr. Norris could say anything, Bud reached for Mr. Norris's plate and took a rib, biting into it, and then put it back on Norris's plate. Bud must not have liked the taste of the ribs, because he took them from his mouth and put them back on Norris's plate as well.

I fell to the ground laughing; I just couldn't believe what had just happened, nor could Mr. Norris, the President. At that point, someone went and got Mama Ella. She was the only person who could get Bud to act right. She took a switch and began to lightly play with it, like popping Bud on his legs. He would act up, but move away from the cag.

Then he would stop dead in his tracks and say she is the only one who can do that. And everyone would just laugh. Bud was a character. That day came to an end, and we got back on the Minute Maid bus and went back to Indiantown from Avon Park.

The very next day, Bud went out on the town, which was a small place called Booker Park. The only problem with him going out was that he strapped his .45 Colt with a nine-inch barrel to his side. Off he goes, with no permit to carry a concealed weapon, and enters Hamp's juke joint, where he sits down at the bar. Orders him a drink after a few shots, and lo and behold, the police walk in - The notorious Charles Jones. He had a reputation for beating people during an arrest; he was known for that.

There, Bud was sitting with the gun scrap on cowboy style, with his Dobb hat tilted slightly to the side on his head. He was wearing a blue surd suit and floor-shine shoes. The police officer Charles Jones walks up to Bud and says, "Hey, old man, what you doin', won't work."

Bud asked him, "What I'm doing?"

Jones said, "You know."

"Give me the gun? Bud said. 'Give you my gun, for what?'

'You are breaking the law if you don't have a permit, so give me the gun.'

Bud looked him in the eye and said, "You got your gun, I got mine, you keep yours because I'm keeping mine."

"Give me the gun," Jones said, before I take it."

" Go head, try an take it. I believe I can draw mine as quick as you can draw yours."

Bud gets up from the seat and walks to his car, then drives home. Charles Jones followed him to his house. There, Bud went to raising hell, saying, "I'm at my house and I don't allow nobody to come here the wrong way, I got a right to having a gun at my house. Now get the h away from my house, you got that?" Charles Jones said, "I'm going to get you, old man." Then he sped off.

⸺⸺✦⸺⸺

Sunday came, and we all went to church. I sat next to the old man, and when the preacher started preaching, the church came alive. A lady was shouting with a big booty, and she was bouncing it all over the place. When she got close to Bud, he frowned up and twisted up his nose as if he smelled a bad odor.

I tried to hold my laugh, but I let it out. He just sat there as if he had done nothing. Then, when the church got quieting down, he let out a thunderous fart, reached over and put his hand on my shoulder, then said, "Don't pay any attention to him, the boy is sick, poor thing. I was so cut down; I never went back to church with him again.

He was the kind of man who believed in trying to have something, so he opened a little café called Uncle Bud's Kitchen on 5th Street, which was the main drag. There, he sold one of the best burgers. Mama Ella was the cook; she would cook dinners all through the week, and mostly burgers on Fridays and Saturdays.

He would sell beer from a cooler out of his van. A person would pay him at the café, then walk over to the van and get the beer from the cooler. That way, he did not have to have a license to sell alcohol.

One night, a really tall black man came to the café and ordered a burger. He sat down and ate it, and then decided he wouldn't pay. He then got nasty with Mama Ella and declared that he was not going to give her a d thing.

Then the man started cursing. Bud then, told the man to get on about his business. But the man being bold stated, "What you gonna do...?" By that time, Bud hit him solid on the side of his head, the gentleman bent over, and Bud bit him on the top of the head. He looked and saw that the man's hair was nappy, unwashed, and just looked ridiculous. Bud went to spitting and gagging, the man went on about his way.

***

Bud and Mama grew older and had to shut down the café. Mama Ella got sugar, which is called diabetes, and lost her legs, then went blind. She lost both her kidneys and had to go on dialysis three days of the week, sometimes four days. Bud was there, and a lady named Virginia met every need. At this point, Bud and Mama had grown old and had been faithful to God and the Christ Church. Once she was sick, the church would not even see about her at all; every now and then, a member would stop by, but that soon stopped.

I am thankful to the good Lord for not only sparing me, but keeping me wrapped in his salvation. It's been a rough life, and yet so good, I just say thank you! I have seen the transition with these eyes and lived it with this life. From picking almost every kind of fruit there is as a migrant worker, moving from place to place.

***

Even though Bud and Momma had grown old and sickly, Bud still was Bud. I had brought my boys a pellet rifle that required pumping up to build pressure until it was as strong as a .22 rifle. Well, one day my wife Terrie caught our son Nazara with the pellet rifle, pointing it at the other boys. They were standing there with their hands up, as if they were under arrest. So Terrie took the gun and gave it to Bud, so the boys could never have another altercation like that.

My cousin Nay was a little off he would go by Bud's place, walk into Bud's house, stick his head in the door, and pick at Bud. Tell him things like "Hey, old man, I ought to come there and put my foot in your ass." He knew that would stir the old man up; he would repeat the same thing over and over. He would stick his head in the door when he would tell Bud this, and step back from the door.

What he didn't realize was that Bud was pumping the pellet gun up, trying to build up as much pressure as he could get in it. Well, Nay must have caught on to something because when Nay saw Little James, he told him Bud said, 'Stick your head in the door; he has something to tell you.'

Little James stuck his head in the door, and the very moment he did, Bud shot him in the forehead. Little James hit the floor, kicking and grabbing his head. Bud jumps out of the bed where he was lying down when he shot James.

He grabs a machete, sees Nay, turns the machete sideways, and starts beating Nay. He's hitting Nay and telling him, 'If you throw your hands up, I'm going to cut them off.' You done made me hurt, James. Bud beat Nay until he ran out of breath.

You would think Nay would have learn a lesson from that. NO. He came back three weeks later, and Bud was in bed. Nay came and stood over him and started talking trash about the beating he had gotten from him. Bud just raised up and shot at his head, but missed him. Nay, shocked from the swiftness, stood there for a moment, then decided to turn to run, but Bud had stuck the pistol a 32 to his thigh and pulled the trigger. Nay falls to the floor and starts to drag his self out of Bud's room.

Momma was blind and could not see, but she heard the shot and Nay. She asked Bud what's that sound I hear, Bud said that's that fool dragging his butt out of here. Nay made it to the center of the street, and a man named Roosevelt said, "You must have been over there messing with Bud." The ambulance picked Nay up and took him to the hospital. That was the life, and the way things were.

As I mentioned in my book "Chicken Scratch", I did not want that for my family; I wanted something better for them.

Well, my sons have become professionals: Architects, Engineers, entrepreneurs, and psychologists. That's a long way from being a migrant worker. My sons are the first in our bloodline to make this vast transition in lifestyle. I stand to give Bud and Mama the honor for that.

The dream of a vision, something hoped for, pleading each and every moment for a disaster not to occur. Nor anything that would derail a family plan for success. Do you know that it's every parent's dream for the next generation to surpass them in terms of progression in life, for the next torch bearer and carrier to have the vision of hope.

"All this is a part of the entrapment".
Trapped in the bubble.

From the heart of man flows all the intent to live, and to live from what is given to him from within. This is evident and physically demonstrated through his achievements in life, which have been consistent over a long period of time, spanning several years. It is not who we claim to be, but who we prove ourselves to be over a given period of time. Only by applying the application of effort was I able to accomplish this goal of restoration. What I mean is that it took guts; it was required of me, despite all the odds stacked up against me. Yet, I was able to survive.

So many have failed and fallen through the cracks of life; they turn to drugs, alcohol, and some even commit suicide from the agony. It's like falling into the hands of an angry God. What in hell did I do for life to turn on me the way it did! By being a survivor of racism and terminal cancer, I wonder so many times myself how I made it this far. To look through these eyes, from this mind, it's a pain to my heart to see so many blind to the facts of life.

See, we are going to live, until we die commonly, by aging, and with all the facets that come with it. I had a vision of hope, love, and happiness for my family, so I worked hard trying to fulfill the dream of success for them. This was something that Mama Ella and Bud instilled in me. As they say, I worked my fingers to the bone. I had been taught by a man who possessed only Mother's wit.

We produced architects, engineers, psychologists, entrepreneurs, doctors, and ministers of the Gospel. All these from the madness of the mind trying to achieve the fulfillment of hope, that one day they too will see an inspirational vision that will drive them the way it drove me, without going over the cliff of life, in the wrong way.

Yes, this trip I've been on is greater than any high; it took me out there into this zone beyond the hallucinogenic reality of thought. Just imagine, grounded with nothing, left there in the wilderness with only a mind and nothing else. The only thing that matters is survival; the million-dollar question is how (to achieve it?).

Something would always tell me to stop, think, and recall the times I had with my mom and Eli, Mama Ella, and the old man Bud. When I was there, all sorts of things flowed through my head, trying to figure it out. Each time I figured up my equations, nothing from nothing leaves nothing. Just another day the lord has blessed me is all I could come up with.

The reason is that someone had to help bring me out of the wilderness; I could not have made this journey by myself. I reckon that is why Mama Ella and Bud were in my life, for me to see life as it is and to keep it real.

JOHN ROBINSON

I was the lead Plaintiff in a civil litigation and was going through all the agony one can imagine. The man I sued, whose name was George Peck Caulkins, was the financial chairman of the Republican Party under the old man Bush administration and a business partner.

Therefore, I was under a lot of pressure from his local supporters, which included the town government and, most of all, those in power. This included the local bank, the First Bank of Indiantown, with whom I did all my banking. I did not know that they were my invisible adversaries who worked for the Caulkins enterprise.

The banker told me to tie a knot in the rope and hold on, because they were about to take me for a ride. This ride would eventually break me down and turn my life into a muddy mess. Bud told me not to ever think of giving up, because the lord was on my side, and a man is nothing but a man, regardless of his standard of *life*.

He also stated that a man bleeds and *got* feelings just like you do. Therefore, just brace yourself and try to withstand the storm; he may not show you any signs that he is worried. But believe me, the man is worried, just from the mere fact of where you got him in the Federal Courts; where every man is on the same level playing field, he has a lot to lose.

Well, things were not working out to well between Bud's land-lord and him, who was his daughter in law. She had two children who were adults on crack, and she just dropped them off at Bud's and told him that they were going to be living there with them. Bud was already catching hell trying to survive with Mama Ella on dialysis. So, he refused to let them stay there, and Minnie raised the rent in retaliation.

That's when I stepped up to the line and told Poppa that he and Mama should move in with us. They moved in and lived, go-ing through the scrutiny of life alongside us. They were with us when we experienced the darkest moments, when I was black-balled in six counties. This included Dade, Broward, Palm Beach, Martin, Okeechobee, and St. Lucie Counties.

No one would hire me. But we had to make it, with no family support, just hang out to dry. Yet Mama had to go to dialysis. We managed to get her treatments. God carried me through these hardships by using a man named Patrick Yancey, the owner of a sanitation company, a garbage hauler. The company's name was All County Sanitation. And a host of fighting attorneys and a dev-astating paralegal.

From the strong tow of this lifeline, I emerged from the dead. Bud would tell me to hold on, boy, God is with you. So glad to catch my breath and get a brand-new look on life, as I thought at this point. I said to myself on many occasions, "I'm thankful to the good Lord for sending somebody to retrieve me. By standing up to fight, without giving up from within and achieving some-thing out of life, be somebody, create somebody by providing a way.

Mr. Yancey became a best friend of mine, and that relationship lasted until the day he died. The family friendship continues to this day. In my book Chicken Scratch, I wrote about being black-balled from six counties.

Trapped in the Bubble.
It's hard to describe what it feels like to be helpless;
it's like being frozen in time, and you can only
feel the freezing effect of it all.

When I was trapped in this bubble, I couldn't move; the only thing I could do was view things outside the bubble. I watched my home being taken because of the lack of funds. I saw all the transportation being picked up or repossessed. I saw my furniture being removed from my home, while being stripped of almost all dignity and pride in the sight of my neighbors

I was *frozen,* rendered and deemed helpless as head of house, the failing father, all this in the presence of my children, whom I taught that all men were created equal. *Trapped in the Bubble:* Locked up, hands tied from deals made while free, with deceitful men of power. The mistake I made was that I gambled with faith, by listening to a banker named Ed Appleton, who gave me relief.

Listen to this if you will. Appleton was the president of the First Bank of Indiantown. He gave me a loan and told me to go out and find a truck that I could use for welding. I ordered a brand new welding machine, in fact, a Lincoln SA 200, which cost around $8,500.00 at the time. I also purchased a set of torches. I got everything I needed to start my business, T&R Mobile Welding Service, a sole proprietor minority business.

Bud would advise me; he would say, "Watch them people, my boy, they are always up to something." Please note that I was blackballed. I didn't have a job at all. An individual introduced by Appleton set me up with a company that was working for the Palm Beach County Solid Waste Authority, the owners of MGM and Universal Studios.

My company became a vendor with them as a Minority firm. Then he told me to tie a knot in the rope and hold on, because they were about to take me for a ride. The problem with me is that I didn't understand what the real deal was all about, concerning money. I thought the money would give me relief, and it would finally be my freedom.

Can you say....
TRAPPED IN THE BUBBLE.

All this and not knowing that he was working with Caulkins, the company I was suing. It was a mind-blowing game. I guess they thought that if I got some relief and was doing very well, I would drop the suit. However, I went out and got certified by Trans Eastern, the company that built the Alaska pipeline. Then I utilized my welding skills and became certified by the Florida Department of Transportation. Now I'm in a position they didn't expect me to be, and this was beyond their expectations.

They really didn't know my abilities because, at Caulkins Citrus Plant, they had no interest in my skills because I was black. Now it's show time for me. I had to demonstrate all my abilities to prove who I am by showing my supreme ability to weld. What I'm saying is that I was among the best in the field of welding, plus I was just as good in the Millwright industry. Even after I rebuilt the plants' feed mill, they were still blinded by my blackness—the color of my skin.

Do you see me...
Trapped in the bubble.

I am a master craftsman when it comes to my skills in the field, and I'm even better at operating a pulp mill. Mr. Ed Appleton had no idea who I was in the industry, nor of my capabilities in terms of my skills. I believe that if he had known at the time of purchase, he would not have given me the loan. Especially if he knew the outcome. That I was going to prevail in the end, they took over $80,000.00 from me for a $20,000.00 loan.

Well, anyway, back to them- before they took the money illegally at the end of the case during the settlement phase, I not only worked for the Solid Waste Authority, but I also became a vendor for Waste Management, the world's largest waste management company.

The types of jobs my company performed for them included refurbishing roll-off tubs, dumpsters, and Garbage Trucks. We rebuilt these units, making them look like new again. For the trucks, we performed a range of tasks, from exchanging hopper liners and cylinders to installing new floors, rebuilding the push, sweep, and carrier blades, and exchanging any form of tracks.

On some of the trucks, we take the high tensile plates and framing apart all the way down to the skeleton of the structure. Then we reconstruct the unit, prime it, and paint it whatever color the owner decided. Normally, it's painted the original color. We completed all the refurbishing work for Waste Management in one half of the State of Florida, from Wildwood to the Georgia line, statewide.

The budget we worked out was $240,000.00 per month, totaling $2,880,000.00 per year. Out of that, my average was about $160,000.00 a month in repairs. We grossed about $1,920,000.00 in repairs. The Waste Management Company seemed to be a great company to work for in terms of race relations. Their color was thinking Green, not about Black or White; it was about moving Garbage. And that's a good thing!

Even though we all were going through some changes, Mama's loss of her legs, and kidneys, plus going blind, we were there all the way for one another. God was there with us; there is no doubt. He used me to show a Giant in life that He was still God. No, it was not about me; it was about God. He used me as the tool to bring the Giant to a recognition of reality. God did it. He gave me the skills, plus the wit from a dead pool of ignorance. He taught me, made me, and kept me.

My company was also a specialist for the State of Florida, having completed projects deemed impossible by the American Welding Society, Law Engineering, and the Department of Transportation itself. For the State, we exchanged or cut out damaged salt-eroded or damaged large beams that supported the bridges. These types of welding repairs were not X-rayed; they were ultrasonically tested. The bridge code is the tightest welding code in existence.

On this one particular project, the Flagler Bridge, in West Palm Beach, Florida, was deemed unrepairable, because the salt erosion had deteriorated the beams at the base, thus leaving the undeteriorated portion of the beam below the surface of the cement of the pier, -which it was poured in during the construction of the bridge.

The problem was, you could only cut an area of six inches around the beam and only three inches deep, making it impossible to repair, they thought. It took the highest-skilled welders in the trade to make this type of repair.

On this project, we cut out and replaced all the damaged beams once we jacked the five-hundred-ton bridge back on grade. You will not believe the company that had the contract was Hagler and Son from Panama, Florida, a neck of the woods where racism was blatant. These fellows had that attitude and tried to meet the Florida DOT's regulations for equality. However, they could not hold up over a long period of time; it would eventually come out. They gave black crew members the name 'Tod', regardless of their name.

This was something I just could not tolerate, so I had all the workers walk off the job in protest. The state would not allow them to work on the bridge; only my team and I, under my supervision, were allowed to repair the major beams, which was what the contract was based on. I had my attorneys negotiate so many hours for us to return to the bridge without any further racist problems, or they would never receive another contract with the State of Florida.

I was able to take care of Bud and Mama from the type of work I was doing. No, Mr. Ed Appleton, nor the Caulkins crew, knew I possessed all these skills. To hell and back I've been from the turmoil they put me through, both physically and mentally. The transition: Born dirt poor, only to be rich in character, stained with pride, and motivated by hope, my life was a mess. It was difficult to find a path from all the twisting and turning, the turmoil life was dumping on me.

But as I mentally held on by faith, believing everything would be alright, I slowly started to heal through the process.

I learned to process the knowledge of the experience, as this experiment of theories flowed through my weak little mind. Hardships are harsh; they break you down or build your strength. In my case, it built my personality to withstand the realities of truth and fact.

One day I went outside and lay down in my front yard, in the middle of the yard in fact, and I decided I would lie there and die. So I lay there, but nothing happened. I kept living, so I said to myself, 'This is reality. I must live until I die.' Then I got up and joined all the family that had gathered around me to see what was wrong.

I got up and said to them, "Wow, a man can't even lie down and die in peace, what a day." We all initially thought it was a funny joke, but it ultimately proved that we had to learn to face facts and move forward in life with a positive mindset. It takes love, dedication, and endurance to navigate life's journey. Well, in 1991, Mama died. Now, that was a sad day for the family. We put her away nicely, and she lives on in us. I had never seen Bud the way he appeared, and the way he took it; he just said that dying is part of living, and we all have to go.

We still fought the trauma we were going through, fighting for justice and equality. Yes, they dealt with me in many ways, trying to create a defense for the case that was court-bound. I was taking them there, come hell or high water; they were going to federal court, if it was within my power to sustain while being Trapped in the Bubble. Bud told me to fight on. We were under federal protection and had an agent from the FBI named Truman. I won the case in court and moved to Valdosta, Georgia. Bud wanted to stay in Florida.

———————

My son and I, along with Fil Corn and his son, welded all the big hunch back, twelve feet by sixty feet, with a five-foot joint fit, beams across the river in St. Mary, GA. This was a project we provided service for the State of Georgia Department of Transportation. We were a certified welding contractor certified by the State of Georgia Department of Transportation.

As I sit here at 3:39 a.m., writing this, I am still amazed at how far the good Lord has brought me.

One day, we got a call saying Bud's leg had to be amputated due to poor circulation. They took off his leg, and I had him brought to Georgia, where he remained for the duration of his life. He hated that they had taken off his leg; he would say to me, 'Boy, look what that B had them do to my leg,' referring to his daughter Janie.

"She knew them people didn't
care anything about no black man."

He was now an 81-year-old man. I would set him in the living room where he could look at the fish pond, which was something he enjoyed doing. I guess it reminded him of the days when he was able to go fishing. Then Bud got sick with a hemorrhaging nosebleed, it was as if a vein had burst. The ambulance came and took him to the hospital, where he remained for a few days.

My wife Terrie, his daughter went to the hospital and picked him up: when they got him in the wheelchair, he said papoo, pa-poo in a way that her mother would call to her. Then he said Ella, slow down, you are walking too fast, talking to his dead wife. When he got to the car, and they were ready to help him out of the wheelchair to be loaded into the car, he said, 'I can do it my-self.' Once he was in the car and had left the hospital, Bud said, while they were riding, "I'm going to eat me a steak wide as both of my hands."

Then he said, 'Stop and buy me a hamburger,' something he had never eaten. He took a big bite, then he let the window of the caddy down and looked up toward the sky, and said, 'Take my hand, Papoo, take it quick.'

Then Bud said, "I'm dying."

Terrie said, "What did he say?"

Coretta answered, "He said I'm dying."

Bud dropped his head and died holding his daughter's hand, while God had him by the other. We put him away as well. I wish he could have lived to see what he done just by being in our lives.

Yet on this day I'm sitting on death row with terminal cancer; I'm in remission. I even beat cancer by the Grace of God and love from and for my family. "What a life for me." I am proud to be able to write to you this testimony, being the witness itself, that all things are possible through faith. You must believe there was someone who was an inspiration in my life.

Yes, I have a lot to contend with. I take shots once a month because my body can't produce sugar; my stomach and pancreas were removed completely. The doctor took my small intestine and created a small eight-ounce pouch called the Hunt Lawrence pouch for my stomach. I had a feeding tube that fed directly into it.

The problem was that God didn't want me to walk around like that, a tube sticking out of my man-made belly, so it just pushed out or came out from back pressure from a nurse trying to flush it clean. She said it's going to be put back once your wounds heal from the surgery. They cut me from the top of my rib cage to my pelvis. The doctor moved my heart over a little in order to cut my esophagus behind my heart to remove my stomach.

Once I underwent that and my surgical wounds healed, I started 42 weeks of chemotherapy and, in addition to 42 treatments of radiation, in a few months. This was a rough ride. My hair fell out, and all my teeth came out, every last one of them. My weight before treatment was 215 pounds, and I went down to a recorded weight of 103 pounds. However, I was even smaller at one point, weighing about 97 pounds, especially when my body was trying to adjust to the new stomach.

I recall during the chemo treatment, scars had developed in my mouth like I had chewed on a mouth full of razor blades. That was very, very painful. They had to prescribe me some numbing medicine to relieve the pain. This lasted for weeks, then it went away.

I would blister up if I went out into the sun because of the type of chemo I was taking. My doctor, Harvey Miller, may not have saved everyone, but he was a significant factor, with his skills, in my life, along with the blessing from God. Do you really want to know the truth and facts of life? Then just face it, racism is equally devastating as this deadly cancer; they both destroy your life. It may at times leave its victims helpless and near dead, hopeless in life, without any reason to live.

My mind should be absolutely shattered from where I am in the bubble, not knowing if or when the deadly cancer will activate itself. It's all over my body, but just lying dormant. The doctors said it's like being asleep. If I contribute to its awakening, it's really a part of my reactions, like worrying over anything. I don't understand exactly what they meant by that, but I hear them loud and clear, so I don't allow anything I mean nothing to worry me.

Now, one thing that I do know and believe with all my heart is that by having Jesus as the head of my life, I need not worry. Look, please don't take that the wrong way. Let's be real and honest: first, it's not about ceremonies, it's about the reality of everyday life for the common person. Believe me, 'The Lord is My Shepherd' will not pay for a loaf of bread; it may get you a free loaf on the street, but not from any store where money is needed for a purchase.

> *Who wants to be in the begging position in life,*
> *for whatever reason! Life is bigger than that.*

It's the politics of politicians that drive things in the wrong direction, leaving many Americans helpless or forcing them into a life of crime due to circumstances. People are different; some are weaker than others. The weaker ones sometimes fall through the cracks in the floor of life, while others get entangled in the fibers of life's carpet.

One of the major factors is the lack of education, as well as limited exposure to mainstream life beyond poverty. Believe me, I know from living below the line of poverty, totally exposed to the underworld. In the underworld, the law is always against you because of the way you are perceived in the eyes of the law.

"The guy that carries the gun".

Will kill you at the blink of an eye if you move a limb, in any manner that he sees as a threatening motion. Even if it's as simple as raising both hands with a cell phone in one hand. He might kill you from fear of the black man syndrome. This syndrome is the unseen factor of fear that some white people have because they've been taught, or have had some horrific experience with black people or a person.

As I said, not all people. I had some Caucasians stand with me in the civil litigation, John Robinson v. Caulkins, Indiantown Citrus Company. They paid a price for standing alongside me; they were fired from their jobs. One individual's pay was cut by $2.00 an hour, just because he took a stand. This underworld exists throughout all black America, even in the business world for blacks.

For small Black entrepreneurs, the scoring system is crucial when it comes to promoting their businesses; 80% always fail, even when the scores are high.

"Can't understand it".

Redlining is sometimes the hidden factor; businesses haven't been in business long enough, even with a constructive business plan. In the city of Valdosta, Georgia, an $ 85,000,000 school was built, with a predominantly black student population, and not one black contractor received a contract. The only black company that was the low bidder was a Company owned by Mr. Terry Kelly, a general contractor.

They took the contract back from him and awarded it to a white-owned company. They never told Mr. Kelly the real reason they took the contract. They believe his bid was too low and never discussed the issue with him. This seems like a repeat of the hardships that have continued from as far back as Bud's time.

There were reasons why his bid was low; he had been misled into thinking he was bidding on only one part of a three-phase project. This occurs frequently with contractors, resulting in their exclusion from federally aided projects. All of this constitutes a violation of federal law, Title 6.

I've seen Black businesses, with a perfect portfolio across the board, be turned down for a standard, common loan by the bank, and the bank grants a loan to the competition of the Black company. Then I see the black business go under, and the owner trying to find work for a typical job in the same field.

That's the intimidating part that we must deal with, the silent frustration of it all. This is the syndrome that plagues the entire black community. This frustration promotes the stigma of not caring. It openly appears in a style of some sort, wearing the pants down, and calling it my swag. *"Do you hear me"?*

Now, coming into play is not combing the hair. What a combination: hair, nappy, and blond, red, blue, or purple; a style to wear your pants down, shirt too big, and wearing Nikes promoting the ' I don't care look'. We lost our pride from the madness of a mentality that was created to destroy us.

The sad part of it all is that some people are falling into the bubble, just to be trapped, because they want to be noticed and classified as something. What happened to the good old days, when the black men, women, and children were driven by the pride of trying to become something in life?

The lack of money in the community, being economically oppressed every day of their lives, time after time, from day to day. Never seeing the light of day from a never-ending night. To be forced to live in darkness, which decays the mind, only to become a navigator of darkness.

"Can you see"?

Its Not a child of light flourishing, in prosperity, living in gated communities, enjoying the absolute best that life has to offer, but born to be bound by the grip of the environment. That's suffocation of life, just to live. To rob, kill, bleed, and then die seems to be the ticket that comes with birth, here in the ghetto, dreams of hope, and the prayers for escape that someday Dr. Martin Luther King's dream will affect their lives.

Oh, Zion what's the matter now.
Is this to black enough for you?

How black do I need to be for you to see into the darkness, as I pray for light. Will this ever end? It looks like the more we struggle to get out, the harder it gets. Yes, we are trapped within this bubble, a bubble of hardships. On top of all of that, we have a president that don't give a damn about us! All he cares about is self-prosperity.

Speaking of the president, George Rhynes and I traveled to Washington, D.C., from March 10th to 14th to attend the NCRC, the National Community Reinvestment Coalition. At this moment, we learned that banks must comply with the requirements to receive the proper grade to obtain money from the Federal government, in order to meet the demands of the CRA.

Many banks only do just enough to comply with federal laws, which do not provide the level of assistance that low-income communities truly need. The old traditional Black communities are still, to this very day, neglected, because of their condition, plagued with poverty. This will never change unless these communities are looked at and accepted as a vital part of a community development program.

These communities can be revitalized by attracting investment to help the community emerge from poverty. It takes money to carry the mail, and the same applies to the community: it takes money. To change the people, you must change their environment, which makes it work for everyone.

When you change the environment, it means that the streetlights change from dim to brighter on the street, and sidewalk improvements occur. Recruitment of new businesses happens, and banking institutions become involved in community renovations by offering loans for home improvements.

All of this is part of the American dream, in the pursuit of happiness and prosperity. The vision of hope is to inspire not only to dream but also to realize the futility of broken promises. The Southside of Valdosta was once a place of prosperous dreams, visions, and hope for tomorrow's children. Especially the ones that evolved from segregation and underwent the transformation of integration in the South. From the struggles I have faced, I hope to achieve my goal of making it better for the loved ones who will come after me and build upon what I leave behind. To see the progression through striving from hard work and the studies of the mind through education.

But that was shattered in 1981 when the James Beck overpass was built; the construction of that bridge literally killed one half of the city. That half was predominantly Black, featuring a variety of black-owned and operated businesses. This was forty years ago, and for those forty years, this community was neglected and excluded from the city's mainstream economic progress.

The vision of hope is still yet alive because we live and believe in the dream. The dream of Justice and equality for all citizens of the Southside, where 40% or more live below the poverty line and 43% earn less than $10,000.00 annually. A place where the soup kitchen is packed every day, churches are overwhelmed by the number of hungry people they feed.

All this is overlooked to the point that it has become the normal way of life, inducing a 'don't care' lifestyle, which is reflected in the litter on the streets. Then, to top it all off, the officials who don't live in the induced conditions of poverty have the audacity to look down on the people. They let it be known by the things they say about how the people live on the southside, instead of trying to search for the solutions, that could alter the cancerous poverty.

Yet the vision of hope remains alive; therefore, we bring forth a structured plan that will restore the Southside. With the conservative effort of all parties working together toward a specific goal, that is to get the Southside back up and running independently. Thus putting in place a real incubator-type system, along with a revolving loan fund, creating a one-stop shop where all or almost all the needs of a community can be met.

A place where a person can start a business and appeal to the city for all the necessary resources to help them achieve their goal. For example, an old, vacant building that is abandoned and just an eyesore. Plan a method of restoration for the building, renovating it to transform into a public gym and business offices for startup businesses.

This is what Bud sparked in us: to take a stand and achieve something in life. Despite what society created within him, look at what he was able to pass on: a vision of hope. A dream that will always dwell within me, and I have already instilled it within all my family members.

He also taught us not to get pissed off, nor pissed on, but keep an umbrella just in case. And they will pass it on. I hope that the reader of this book understands why I seem to have skipped around with my topics, while touching on the lives, views, and actions of those who were and are *trapped in the bubble.*

I wrote in this manner to make you wonder about the mentality of a black man and how it can be driven to react.

May God Bless You.
We are just TRAPPED IN THE BUBBLE.

THE FLOWER

Drawn by a 13 yr old whose inspired by art. *D.J.R.*

www.ingramcontent.com/pod-product-compliance
Lightning Source LLC
Chambersburg PA
CBHW031428120626
46545CB00006B/2319